W9-ACE-995

WITHDRAWN

WILLIAM GRANT STILL

AMERICAN

Composers

A list of books in the series
appears at the end of this book.

William
Grant Still

Catherine Parsons Smith

UNIVERSITY OF
ILLINOIS PRESS
Urbana and Chicago

© 2008 by the
Board of Trustees
of the University
of Illinois
All rights reserved
Manufactured in the
United States of America

♾ This book is printed
on acid-free paper.

c 5 4 3 2 1

Library of Congress Cataloging-in-Publication Data
Smith, Catherine Parsons, 1933–
William Grant Still / Catherine Parsons Smith.
p. cm. — (American composers)
Includes bibliographical references (p.),
discography (p.), and index.
ISBN-13 978-0-252-03322-3 (cloth : alk. paper)
ISBN-10 0-252-03322-1 (cloth : alk. paper)
1. Still, William Grant, 1895–1978.
2. African American composers—Biography.
I. Title.
ML410.S855S64   2008
780.92—dc22 [B]   2007044085

Still, c. 1930. Irving Schwerké arranged for several performances of Still's music in Europe over the next few years. Music Division, The New York Public Library for the Performing Arts, Astor, Lenox and Tilden Foundations. Used by permission.

CONTENTS

PREFACE

LONG BEFORE I THOUGHT TO WRITE ABOUT William Grant Still, I interviewed his widow, Verna Arvey, in connection with another project. Arvey was a rich source of information about music making in Los Angeles, about her own career, and about her famous husband. Had I had more foresight, I would have asked many more questions about him then, for the chance to ask them did not recur. Other family members, however, have provided information, answered questions, and encouraged me to speak and write about him. For example, there was an invitation to write an essay on Still's years in Los Angeles for a conference and a volume on music in the city's Central Avenue community. Another such opportunity was to organize the paper sessions and help arrange the performances at a three-day Still festival at Northern Arizona University in 1998. In addition to several journal articles, there was a volume of essays and previously unpublished sources addressing issues and individuals around Still, concentrating on the decade of the 1930s. But, until now I have not attempted a biography.

The University of Illinois Press's new American Composers series provides an opportunity for an overview of this remarkable composer's career. The main results of this new approach to the sources are a fuller description of Still's early career in Ohio and New York, and a more careful look at the circumstances around the 1949 production of his opera *Troubled Island*. But those things are far from the whole story, either about Still himself or the place of his body of work in our culture. Among other things, Still's career forces us to rethink conventional assumptions about race and concert music in America. The significance of his artistic achievement makes this and future reexaminations well worth the effort. Even more important, it makes a compelling argument for more performances of his music, including new productions of his operas.

An advance from the University of Illinois Press and a Dena Epstein Award from the Music Library Association facilitated renewed research in collections in

Little Rock, Arkansas, and at the University of Arkansas–Fayetteville. Librarians and archivists in both places, and at my home library at the University of Nevada–Reno, have been unfailingly helpful. In the past, I have consulted the collection at William Grant Still Music in Flagstaff, Arizona, to good effect, though not for this project. Permission could not be obtained for a CD to accompany this volume. Fortunately, many readers have access to online download services, where they may find everything that might have been on such a CD and much more besides. Because the photographs in the Still-Arvey collection at the University of Arkansas–Fayetteville are unavailable to me at this writing, I am especially grateful to the American Memory online archive of the Library of Congress, the Hogan Jazz Archive of Tulane University, and the Library for the Performing Arts and the Schomburg Center for Research in Black Culture of the New York Public Library, the Hollywood Bowl Museum, the Los Angeles Music Center Archive, the Sibley Library of the Eastman School of Music, Cambria Archives, Elliott Hurwitt, Sara Moore Cummings, Judy McCulloh, and the Museum of the City of New York for their advice and assistance in obtaining illustrations. I am grateful to Still's associates, friends, and family members who have given interviews over a period of years, in person, by telephone, and through e-mail. In addition, several readers have made valuable suggestions; in particular, I thank Paul Charosh, Gayle Murchison, Wayne Shirley, and Josephine Wright, as well as my readers and editors at the University of Illinois Press.

A NOTE ON RESEARCH

THE WILLIAM GRANT STILL–VERNA ARVEY PAPERS at the University of Arkansas–Fayetteville, Department of Special Collections (hereafter UAF), is the principal primary resource for research on Still. Its coverage is fullest after 1934. A detailed finding aid is available online at http://libinfo.uark.edu/ SpecialCollections/findingaids/still/still1aid.html. Additional materials are located at William Grant Still Music in Flagstaff, Ariz.; access to this source is limited.

Some points about the Still-Arvey Papers at UAF may be helpful for future researchers. Not all the letters from significant people in his life are in the folders designated for them. Researchers should consult the "miscellaneous" folders at the end of each alphabetical category. In addition, some letters are filed under the names of their writers, and others are filed under their institutions or businesses. (For Howard Hanson, for example, one should look at both "Hanson" and "H" miscellaneous, as well as "Eastman School of Music," "University of Rochester," and "E" and "U" miscellaneous.) Materials added to the collection after it was initially processed may not be listed in the finding aid. Researchers should specifically request a list of materials added later.

In supplementing those primary collections with other resources, I have privileged earlier sources over later ones. For example, I have depended more heavily on Still's "Personal Notes," written by him in 1932 or 1933, than on Arvey's later *In One Lifetime* (Fayetteville: University of Arkansas Press, 1984). No researcher can escape Arvey's influence on the Still legacy, but I have attempted to balance it through the use of earlier sources and materials in related collections, as well as through personal interviews.

Still in 1949. Library of Congress, Prints & Photographs Division, Carl Van Vechten Collection (Reproduction Number LC-USZ62-103930).

WILLIAM GRANT STILL

I | An Uncertain
Ovation

ON THE EVENING of March 31, 1949, a large audience filled the City Center for Music and Drama in midtown Manhattan for an operatic premiere that, to the heartfelt satisfaction of most of the audience, broke two of the major color barriers around opera in mid-twentieth-century America. An African American composer and an African American poet/librettist, each already prominent as creative artists, were about to be heard in a major American opera house, an achievement so unusual that it would not happen again for almost forty years (not until 1986, with Anthony Davis's *X, The Life and Times of Malcolm X*, also produced by the New York City Opera. No African American would sing at the Metropolitan Opera for another six years).

At the end of the performance, there was an ovation. The elated composer, William Grant Still, took six curtain calls alongside the cast and conductor. Yet his satisfaction proved fleeting. Indicative of the problems that had already arisen, the librettist, Langston Hughes, did not join him onstage and missed the post-performance celebration altogether.

Like most other African American musicians, Still had sustained himself by working as a performer and arranger in clubs and in musical theater. Unlike many of them, he had worked steadfastly toward recognition as a composer of opera for most of his fifty-four years. The commercial work and the extensive achievements

2

with concert music, including the splendid symphonic suite *Africa*, the famous *Afro-American Symphony*, the ballet *Sahdji*, and his World's Fair music had been ear-catching way stations, warm-ups for this moment.

How did Still reach that moment at the New York City Opera? And how is it that an African American composer chose to express his talent through concert music and opera rather than the more "popular" genres, anyway? That is not as unusual as it may seem at first glance. Still was in fact following a well-established tradition of black involvement in opera, albeit one that has been overshadowed by the enormous success of black-influenced popular and commercial music.[1]

This last question is actually something of a red herring, for it has kept us from getting to some more basic questions. Could a similarly talented man of Still's generation, one with a different ethnic or racial identity—an American male with an Anglo-Saxon, or Jewish, or Native American, or Asian background—have produced the same or a similarly oriented body of work? My argument here is, unequivocally no. Then we must ask, if his music was indeed unique and fundamentally "authentic," as I claim, then how did Still go about expressing his position in American culture and society through his creative work, given that he abandoned the commercial field in which African Americans have been so successful?

The uniqueness of Still's contribution includes the titles and the subjects he chose to write about, but it goes far beyond them, reaching to the heart of his musical style. It lies in the ways he built on African American traditions to speak in a genuinely new voice, and to a wide, multi-ethnic concert- and opera-going population. And if I am right about this, we have a thoroughly convincing answer to the claim made occasionally that by composing concert music, Still was somehow not composing himself. In fact, he was expressing the ambivalences of his position in the culture with devastating effectiveness. It now seems strange, given this position, that Still and his main public spokesperson chose to emphasize the "American" part of his contribution rather than the African American cultural elements that lent it its distinctive character, making it easier for critics to miss the newness—as well as the "blackness"—of his musical speech.

To get down to cases, the subject of *Troubled Island*, the work performed on that evening in 1949, is the revolution of 1791 that ended the practice of slavery in Haiti long before the Emancipation Proclamation ended it in the United States. Turning on racial violence as well as intrigue and personal tragedy, the plot was—and still is—a provocative one for an opera. That was so even for the overwhelmingly white, generally liberal middle- and working-class audience drawn to the New York City Opera, an unusually egalitarian opera house in those early days. The contrasting responses of composer and librettist (both relatively light-skinned African Americans, members of W. E. B. Du Bois's "talented tenth" by virtue of their education and achievements) to the opera's premiere reflect the ambivalence that has surrounded this opera and, more generally, Still's extensive body of work as a composer of operas and concert music. The aftermath, like other aspects of Still's career, had much to do with contemporary political events, class issues associated with music, musical politics, and, as is so often the case in American culture, pervasive, almost overwhelming race-based expectations and stereotypes.

As both prelude and accompaniment to greater insight into his musical style, then, I set out to understand what we can know of the man and the circumstances that led him to do what he did. This book is about how Still built on traditions of African American and American music as he found them, then moved through a series of breakthroughs and firsts as a composer and conductor to arrive at that triumphant moment in 1949, and what happened afterward. The story, like the person who is its subject, is complex. Still was a gifted, resourceful, private, fiercely determined individual who wove a unique path through the racial and cultural thickets of his time to create a generally excellent, still-viable body of music. He composed ballets and symphonic works, as well as operas, songs, and chamber music, over a lengthy career. We continue to hear a few of the many works he created, mostly nowadays the *Afro-American Symphony* during Black History Month. The book will have succeeded if it provokes new and continuing discussion and understanding of his contributions and his place in our collective cultural history.

I set the scene by going back to a time before young Billy Still, 1911 graduate of segregated M. W. Gibbs (later Dunbar) High School in Little Rock, Arkansas, decided to pursue his dream of becoming a composer of concert music and opera, in a place and at a time when music thrived—in bars, theaters, churches, and brothels—but was well-nigh unimaginable as an appropriate principal occupation for an educated, ambitious young man of color from a respectable Southern family.

2 | Still's Arkansas Childhood

Family Background

William Still Sr. and Carrie Fambro, the composer's parents, grew to adulthood in the 1880s, a time when the promises of Emancipation and Reconstruction were already shrinking. Each of them, one in Mississippi and the other in Georgia, was heir to certain advantages that brought a degree of opportunity and marginal privilege within the widespread system of repression under which all African Americans lived. The privilege came from several circumstances. Three of the composer's four grandparents had been free even before Emancipation, and the fourth, Carrie's mother, had been a house slave. Their skins were relatively light, elevating them automatically within the prevailing hierarchy of color among African Americans.

Like Carrie's mother, Ann[e] Fambro, Duncan and Mary Still (William's parents) are both listed as "mulatto" in the 1880 Census. (Carrie's father is not mentioned, which is consistent with the family lore that has him as white.) Their relative distance from slavery and their light skin color outweighed the fact that neither Mary nor Anne could read or write; thus, some doors for self-advancement were slightly open for both William Sr. and Carrie. In addition, strong family ties on both sides provided a support system that was key in a time when student loans and publicly funded social support did not exist. Added to that, both of the composer's future parents aggressively sought out formal education for themselves. Both managed to acquire teaching credentials ("normal" diplomas, in the language of the time) and both became teachers, a high-status (if ill-paid) profession among blacks.

Neither Mississippi nor Georgia in the 1890s, the time of William and Carrie's young adulthood, was all that promising a place for anyone, regardless of race. Before the Civil War, literacy rates had been low among whites, and reading had been illegal for blacks. After the destruction caused by the war and the collapse of the slave-subsidized cotton economy, the Southern states and counties provided only minimal public education for their white population. They offered significantly less for blacks. The school year was short, and shorter yet for blacks. High schools for black students were few and far between. The "separate but equal" school systems made permanent by the Supreme Court's *Plessy v. Ferguson* decision in 1896 were notoriously unequal and did not improve. Racial discrimination was increasingly formalized by "Jim Crow" segregation laws, many of which were not passed until after 1890. The reality of random, semiofficial violence against people of color had a dampening effect as well. All this made the level of education achieved by Still's parents more remarkable, underlining their good fortune in being able to take advantage of what their limited privilege allowed.[1]

Census records amplify the family lore passed along by the composer and written down much later. Grandfather Duncan Still and his wife, Mary, were farmers in Wilkinson County, Mississippi. In 1887 they became the owners of ninety-three acres of gently rolling farmland, close to the Louisiana state line and a few miles from the Mississippi River. The fact of ownership is unusual, for most blacks were sharecroppers, working rented land. Duncan Still's family connection with a much wealthier, white Still family in the area may explain this. Courthouse records show that Duncan and Mary regularly mortgaged their farm in the spring to raise money to plant their crops, then paid it off in the fall, after the harvest.[2] Sometimes they brought witnesses to the Woodville courthouse in order to assure that they were not unwittingly signing away their land. Duncan signed, and Mary, who is said to have been half Native American, made her mark.

In the 1880 Census, their son William, the composer's father, was said to be nine years old. Like his two teenage sisters, he is listed as a farmhand, a customary designation for any black child over five years of age. William became a good deal more than a farmhand, however. He learned to read and showed a good head for numbers. Musically talented, he traveled some distance to pursue cornet lessons. He also organized a band. Family lore says that he was a partner in a store as well. William presently attended Alcorn A&M in nearby Lorman, one of the new colleges for African Americans, graduating in 1892. He then taught bookkeeping and music at Alabama A&I in Normal, Alabama, where one of his successors was W. C. Handy. (The traditionally black colleges all had large preparatory departments to make up for the lack of access to public high schools. Their records are spotty to nonexistent; thus, it is hard to be certain at what levels either he or Carrie studied and taught.) Altogether, William was a promising young man.

Still's mother was Carrie Fambro, born and raised in Pike County, Georgia, where the name Fambro/Fambrough was claimed by both white and black families. The informative 1880 Census lists her as fifteen years old and already a schoolteacher. Along with her mother (Anne Fambro), she and three sisters (Ocia/Ocie, Laura, Eliza) lived in the household of twenty-nine-year-old Romeo Maxey, principal of the Union Colored School in Barnesville. All were listed as mulatto. Maxey and Ocia were married; their two small children completed the household. Anne Fambro, the grandmother who helped raise Still and always lived with her daughters, is listed in 1880 as a dressmaker, a skilled and essential occupation in a culture devoid of ready-made clothing. Family lore says she kept a boardinghouse and worked as a cook. Illiterate herself, she strongly encouraged her children's—and later her grandson's—education.

Young Carrie was both able and ambitious. Having begun to teach by age fifteen, she must have combined her own studies with teaching over a good many years to gain her degree. Family lore says she played the organ in a church in Barnesville for a time. Her degree from Atlanta University is dated 1886. (Carrie chiseled a few years from her age over the next several censuses. It is likely that she made herself younger so she could keep teaching as long as possible, for age discrimination was rampant, and pensions for black teachers were either non-existent or much lower than for whites. Unaware of this adjustment, the family gives her birth year as 1873; it was probably closer to 1865.)

We lose track of Carrie Fambro for a few years after her graduation in 1886. In 1893–94, however, she was teaching at Alabama A&I in Normal, Alabama. That was the year that William Still Sr. arrived there to teach. The couple soon married and moved back to Woodville, his hometown. There Carrie taught at Bayridge Church and William taught at Chapel Church. William also taught at Steward (not further identified), and was principal at a school in Gloster until it closed abruptly in the face of deadly white violence against its other teacher. William Grant Still Jr., the future composer, was born on May 11, 1895. The following September, when the baby was four months old, his father's promise came to an early end. William Sr. died of a mysterious fever, probably malaria or yellow fever, thought to be poison by some of his descendants. The composer's later account of his father's death hints at some of the religious ideas embedded in his cultural inheritance:

> My mother related some unusual occurrences connected with his death. . . . One was that an owl persisted in perching on the roof of the house despite all efforts to drive him away. If I remember correctly the bird remained there for a number of days, and would not leave until my father had died. It would not seem strange were it not for the old superstition concerning owls and death.—My mother also told me of the beautiful vision my father had when he was expiring . . . Just before he passed out he rose in bed and told those present of an angelic being that he saw approaching him. He described this beautiful entity to them, telling them that it was coming for him and then died.[3]

(This quotation, and several others concerning his early years, come from the "Personal Notes" Still wrote at the request of Harold Bruce Forsythe, who had proposed a biography of Still. It is the earliest and most reliable autobiographical account we have.) Still acknowledges the existence of "the old superstition," though he keeps it at arm's length in this narrative. But, by the time he wrote that account (probably in late 1932), he had recorded descriptions of visions of his own. In the early 1920s, his strong spirituality linked him to African American cultural traditions. It also gave him an important way to connect with many white composers and musicians, through a common interest in popular forms of spiritualism. Still's religious conviction remained ingrained in his character, even though he had no traceable church membership in the course of his adult life. We can see it in the title and the orchestration of such works as *From the Land of Dreams*. Later it proved significant as he articulated the aesthetic ideas that underlay other works as well.

Little Rock

Suddenly deprived of the hopes that had taken her to the rural Woodville area with her husband, Carrie executed a guardianship agreement for the farm (which had passed by law to Baby Will) and went within months to live in Little Rock, Arkansas, where her sister Laura, now married, and her mother had settled. She made the move not only because of her family connection. Woodville had a violent history and did not support its black school system well; to remain there was to be assured of a life of uncertainty and poverty, for her son as well as for herself. Little Rock, on the other hand, was known in the 1890s as one of the more enlightened, cosmopolitan, and generally desirable cities in the South for African Americans. (This would change later.) Its black population could still vote.

There were a fair-sized black middle class and a growing number of black-owned businesses and churches. Most important of all, there was a high school for black students. Carrie's opportunity to teach would be more secure, and, when her son was ready, he would have access to an education, even though it was in a segregated school system with severely limited resources.

City directories show that Carrie and Baby Will, as he was called at first, lived with his grandmother Fambro, his aunt Laura Fambro Oliver, and Laura's husband, Henry, a barber, in a house at 912 West Fourteenth Street. The composer's recollections do not include living with his mother's extended family, yet he lived at that address until he left home in 1911, and Carrie remained there throughout her life, eventually replacing her sister as the owner.[4]

Among her other activities in Little Rock, Carrie is credited with leading the drive to organize a lending library (at the black school) that was open to the black population; she was also active in the women's club movement. Segregation was not practiced as rigidly in the Little Rock of Still's youth as it later was, though the situation steadily worsened. It was not until 1903, for example, when Still was eight years old, that the public bus system was formally segregated. Carrie was among the resistors, participating in a "We Walk League." African American families lived on either side of Still's home, yet he remembered the neighborhood as racially mixed and recalled several white playmates. Despite the inconveniences and the barriers, he later spoke of his boyhood as a relatively normal one for an American of his time and place. Be that as it may, he came to his lifelong conviction that deliberate racial separatism was a negative value in these early years.

Still attended Capitol Hill school, which at first was a combined elementary and secondary school. Later he attended Union School for one or two years, the eighth grade and maybe the ninth. When the separate, segregated high school opened, Still was a student in his mother's English classes, where Shakespeare was part of the curriculum. To motivate her students, she wrote and produced school plays, including some that were given in a downtown theater. (Local blacks remembered those "extravaganzas" fondly. Among other things, the all-black audience, liberated from its usual confinement to the balcony, got a chance to sit anywhere in the theater.[5]) She insisted that Still learn to think in addition to achieving academically: "I had to be [high school valedictorian] because my mother made up her mind that I must be, and she made me study. She would never work out any problems that presented themselves for me but would force me to work them out for myself."[6] Still's high school graduating class included twenty-six women but only nine men. He later wrote that many of the male students had dropped out before graduating, mostly to help their families by going to work. His persistence, and Carrie's encouragement, is another indication of his relative privilege as well as his ability.

Wrapped up in her teaching and her community activism as she was, Carrie nevertheless provided a loving but firm environment for young Billy, who was glad to throw off the old "Baby Will" label as soon as he could. She did her best to keep a tight rein on him. From all accounts, he did not hesitate to test her limits, and she did not hesitate to enforce them. He wrote the following after he had children of his own and his early first marriage had disintegrated:

> My mother had high aims for me, and she started working toward them, i.e. molding my method of thought at a very early age. I had to read the books she chose—and I'm grateful to her now for it. She constantly impressed me with the thought that I should achieve something worth while in life. She sought to aid me [to] reach the state of mind that leaves one unhappy when he has failed to put forth his best effort. She wanted me to be a man and, for that reason, dealt with me in a manner that would have seemed strange to some mothers who are inclined to coddle their children. But my mother knew what I needed, and I am thankful for it. She sought at all times to give me every advantage that she possibly could. (I rarely missed passing through a day without a licking. But I needed them. Had my mother not employed that means of teaching me to control myself I don't know what the results would have been. Certainly with such a stubborn will as mine things would have gone wrong somewhere.)[7]

His mother's tough love was reinforced and balanced by his grandmother Fambro's more indulgent affection. She was devoted to Still, and Still to her. In the same "Personal Notes" quoted above, he wrote of her:

> I spent much of my time in childhood around my maternal grandmother. I have much to thank her for. She was one of the old fashioned devout Christians. She had been a slave, although she was one of the fortunate ones who did not have to work in the fields. . . . She knew and sang the old songs that voiced the slaves' belief that God would not forget them. Because of her influence I have been enabled to realize the value of things spiritual, and to love them. . . . God was good to me to give me such a grandmother. She loved me . . . Each day when I would come home from school she would have something special prepared for me. Pies, cookies, candy or something good that she had made . . .[8]

When Still was nine, Carrie married Charles B. Shepperson, a railway mail clerk. Shepperson was a good choice from the boy's point of view: "In truth, a father could not have been more considerate. He and I spent many pleasant and profitable moments together. He too liked music. [I] learned at an early age to appreciate the better sort of music through the records he would buy."[9] Shepperson encouraged Carrie to allow Still violin lessons when he reached high school age, after he had made an instrument of his own from a cigar box. The lessons seem not to have lasted very long. The lack of earlier music instruction, especially on the violin, probably hindered him later on, when he needed to earn a living as a performer. A certain diffidence about performing, part of his fundamentally private character, was probably reinforced by this lack.

On the other hand, even without encouragement, as soon as he learned how to read music, the boy attempted to write down his own, often concealing his efforts from his parents. (None of these early efforts survive.) The quiet, single-minded determination that becomes in hindsight the most prominent feature of his character was the result of both his inherited nature and the nurture he drew from his early environment. When he was in his forties, his friend Forsythe noted, "Those who knew him as a child remark concerning the exceptional shyness and reserve of his manner, and his stubborn resolution."[10] The stubbornness put him in frequent conflict with Carrie. One imagines efforts at mediation from Grandmother Fambro and Mr. Shepperson. Carrie's model—a strong and determined woman with her own convictions about his best interests, along with his tendency to accept her judgment—was a powerful influence throughout his life.

Another statement from Still's 1932 "Personal Notes" is indicative of an aspect of his early conditioning that he thought important all those years later. "In me the fleshly tendencies are strong," he wrote. "Were it not for the training I received through contact with my grandmother I could not restrain them."[11]

Current Events

The competing ideas expressed in the long-running debate between Booker T. Washington, the "sage of Tuskegee," and his somewhat younger critic, W. E. B. Du Bois, over how best African Americans should improve their lot, got started in Still's childhood and were highly relevant to his life. The debate began with Washington's 1893 "Atlanta" speech and continued for decades after Du Bois responded with *The Souls of Black Folk* (1903).[12] Washington urged Southerners, black and white, to "cast down your bucket where you are" (a phrase echoed many years later by Still's second wife, Verna Arvey, a lifelong Los Angeles resident, referring to her decision to remain where she was) to make conditions better for all. Washington believed that progress toward full citizenship would be gradual, that it would be granted willingly by whites as blacks became better educated. When young Still aspired briefly to become a chicken farmer, he was responding to one of Washington's Little Rock speeches. (Washington came to Little Rock at least twice while Still was growing up, once in 1906 and again in 1911, speaking to large audiences both times; he remarked on the economic and cultural successes of the city's black population, which were unusual in the South.)

Washington's acceptance of social segregation and the limitations he advocated for the education of black Americans drew criticism, led by the younger W. E. B. Du Bois. Yet parts of Washington's message resonated in the minds of many educated people in the coming decades, including the Stills. He argued that segregationists acted through ignorance, needing only education and enlightenment to change their ways voluntarily, a position Still echoed in the 1960s as he developed a strong antipathy to the black activists of a later generation who had lost touch—and patience—with this argument.

In practice, Carrie, and later her son, followed precepts embraced by both leaders. Despite the publicity and influence that Washington achieved in Little Rock, Carrie remained convinced that academic achievement knew no racial boundaries. Thus she sided in practice with Du Bois when it came to academic standards. Those high standards had long paid off for Little Rock's black population. Several of its citizens had successfully pursued the study of medicine, dentistry, and other professions at Oberlin, Harvard, and other northern universities, then returned to practice their professions in the city. (Among these was the dentist James H. Smith, whose daughter, Florence Price, several years older than Still, studied at the New England Conservatory, then returned to Little Rock for some years of teaching before joining the northern exodus—actually fleeing a specific threat of violence—and moving to Chicago in the mid-1920s to pursue her own career of performing, teaching, and composing.) Carrie became secretary of the NAACP (National Association for the Advancement of Colored People, founded by Du Bois, among others) chapter when it was organized in Little Rock, very likely a part of her protest against the growing loss of opportunity for her students.

Washington's advocacy of vocational education had a very real effect on the black school system in Little Rock, for it reinforced a reaction against the impulse that had led to the building of the black high school Still attended. As Still was approaching graduation, the school board was preparing to drop much of Gibbs's academic program in favor of vocational education. Newspaper accounts from 1910 and 1912 report petitions from the black community to the local board of education not to drop the courses in German, Latin, trigonometry, chemistry, and biology that were then offered. The paper added editorially that such education courses "spoiled" blacks for work even more often than they "spoiled" whites.[13] Carrie was forced to watch the program that had brought opportunity for her son systematically dismantled, limiting her later students to the new vocational program that replaced it. Her pressure on Still to do well and seek further education elsewhere becomes all the more understandable in the light of these negative developments.

Exposure to Music

Still heard music at home and in the community. Grandmother Fambro sang spirituals; the family sang hymns in the upper-class black (Presbyterian) church they attended. Presently Mr. Shepperson took Still to hear and see touring black artists such as the violinist Clarence Cameron White, soprano Azalia Hackley, and Shakespearean actor Richard B. Harrison. Still's later accounts have his early hearings of recorded operatic excerpts as one of the formative events in his young life. It is not clear when he first heard them, though he reports that he was greatly affected by them after he had entered college.

Apart from Grandmother Fambro's singing at home and an occasional trip with his mother, who used some of her school "vacation" time to teach basic literacy in nearby rural black churches, Still had little exposure to vernacular black religious practices or the music that was integral to them. Still's interest in music was clear, however, and so was his mother's opposition to his pursuing it as a career. Black musicians performed irregularly, in disreputable locations, and for little pay. Music, to be sure, was one of the professions open to people of color, but it was not regarded as a desirable career or one that would allow young Still to serve the race as she was preparing him to do. Perhaps her conviction was reinforced by the fate of her first husband, William Still Sr. Their conflict over this came to a head after Still's first year of college; it must have remained a sore point between them for a long time.

After Still had left home, there was a modicum of prosperity. The Sheppersons had enough money to invest $800, almost two years' salary for Carrie, in some Arkansas oil leases around 1918, as well as to buy the house they had lived in for so long, along with a large lot nearby, later subdivided into five building lots. Only a few years later, however, Mr. Shepperson, who was then about fifty, died suddenly. His death—by drowning in a shallow pond, possibly a cesspool—is invariably reported as an accident.[14] One wonders, though, whether racial violence played a part.

Carrie died of cancer in 1927. In her will, she left only token amounts to her sisters Laura and Eliza (despite Laura's early generosity) and to Mr. Shepperson's many siblings (who received the worthless oil leases.) Most of her estate was left to her son and her sister Ocia.[15] Still seems to have garnered very little benefit from the family's property, however. What he did take away from Little Rock was his quiet determination, his high expectations for himself, the powerful influence of his grandmother's "old fashioned devout Christian[ity]," his perennial struggle for self-control, and an image of the ideal woman as a strong-willed, caring individual, supportive, with intellectual, and especially literary, interests.

3 | An Ohio
Apprenticeship

GRADUATING FROM HIGH SCHOOL soon after his sixteenth birthday, Still followed his mother's wishes and enrolled at Wilberforce University, near Dayton, Ohio. Founded seven years before Emancipation, Wilberforce's strict Christian orientation was tailored to teach self-sufficiency and racial pride to its students, and to communicate a sense of black achievement and gentility to the wider white community. Daily chapel for all and military drill for the men were standard. A strict code of sexual behavior, part of a program designed to demonstrate that people of color did not fit the stereotype of "an ignorant and immoral race," as one of their early presidents put it, was rigidly enforced. Female students had to be chaperoned at all times, including at choir rehearsals and en route to the railroad station at vacation time. They were not even allowed to walk from class to class without supervision. (Much of the chaperoning duty fell to the women faculty, who found it onerous.) The faculty gave only grudging approval to occasional extracurricular activities, including a handful of concerts given by students and by visitors from outside.

The school offered three programs at the time Still was a student there; music was not among them. There was an Academy for the many students who came without sufficient preparation for college. (Still's academic opportunity had indeed been unusually strong, thanks to his mother.) A two-year Combined Normal and

Industrial (CN&I) program for teacher training was financially supported from 1887 until the 1940s by the state of Ohio. Still was enrolled in the third program, a four-year academic course leading toward the BS degree. A much later letter from the registrar reports, "He took several courses in German, French, Latin, Mathematics, Biology, English, Physics and Philosophy."[1] Still himself wrote only briefly of his college years in his "Personal Notes." We learn there that a major confrontation with his mother over his career path took place shortly after his seventeenth birthday, between his first and second years at Wilberforce. Stimulated by the opera recordings that Mr. Shepperson brought home, his commitment to music as a profession came irrevocably out of hiding at that point. His fascination with both opera and the technology that had brought its sound into his family's home could no longer be concealed.

> After having completed high school I was sent to Wilberforce. There I was thrown in contact with some fellows who were lovers of music. These contacts were helpful.[2]
>
> Upon returning home after my first year at college I begged my mother to send me to Oberlin. But she had mapped out a career for me. I was to finish Wilberforce and then go to Oxford. That did not interest me. I wanted to study music. And so I wasted time in college just barely making my grades; always in trouble for playing pranks; spending most of my time studying music, attempting to write and playing the violin . . .[3]

Still's own report reveals that his mother won the initial battle. He returned to Wilberforce in the fall as she wished, but from that point on he systematically practiced passive resistance toward the academic aspirations she had so carefully encouraged. When he was ready, or maybe a little before that moment, he found a way to firmly close the door on her ambitions.

In the absence of any formal music curriculum, Still invented his own independent study program, spending his allowance on opera scores and throwing himself into whatever music activities he could find or devise. In place of the military drill, he joined a newly formed band, sometimes leading it himself, and eventually teaching himself to play oboe, clarinet, 'cello, saxophone, and piccolo well enough to understand their capabilities and teach them to prospective band members. He organized a string quartet too, and made arrangements for both groups. Occasionally he went with faculty to hear concerts in nearby Dayton, where the Cincinnati Symphony played regularly, and where traveling opera companies and concert artists also performed. The Afro-British composer Samuel Coleridge-Taylor, who visited the United States several times before his death in 1912, became an important role model. (It is unlikely that Still was able to meet him.) When the violinist Clarence Cameron White performed on campus, he offered words of encouragement to young Still. Some faculty members and their wives also encouraged him and even played his compositions for him. One photograph from those years shows Still as a member of the string quartet. Another, in the 1914 college yearbook (the only one from his years to survive), shows him seated with a 'cello, looking smaller and younger than the other members of the school "orchestra" as all seven of them sit in a single line in front of the men's glee club. The same yearbook lists a concert program made up entirely of Still's compositions, scheduled for May 1914. None of the works on that list survives, and there is some reason to doubt that the concert actually took place, as will become clear. Verna Arvey's later statement that Still found more musical activity at Wilberforce than before may be true, but it does not reflect his impatience and dissatisfaction with his program there.

Accounts of how Still came to leave school in his senior year, without graduating, are mysterious. Still wrote: "Finally in my senior year, just about six weeks before I would have graduated I got mixed up in another prank. This was of a more serious nature—to be exact it appeared serious to others although nothing was [done] by any concerned that was at all wrong, i.e. morally."[4] Later family

Glee Club and Orchestra, Wilberforce University, 1914. Still is seated at the left, holding his 'cello. Tawawa Remembrancer, *1914, p. 43.*

narratives tell us that Still joined a group of students for an illegal picnic and walk in the nearby woods, and that Grace Bundy, whose name had not previously been associated with his, was his partner. Faculty members surprised them before they got off campus. Fearing dismissal, Still packed his things and left Wilberforce behind permanently; the others were, apparently, expelled. The only verification for this story, and a powerful one, is that a few months later (October 1915), Still married Ms. Bundy, who within a few months went home to her family in Kentucky. Their first child, William Bundy Still, was born the following fall. Thereafter Still was concerned to support his new family, a heavy consideration. Her presence, and her influence on Still, figure more strongly later on, during their years in New York. Still wrote later only that his mother was disappointed in his decision to marry as well as in his premature departure from Wilberforce.

School records are sparse from Still's time. Apart from the 1936 registrar's letter, no record of what he studied or what grades he earned has been located. What do survive are two bound volumes of minutes from faculty meetings covering the years when he was enrolled. For most of that time, the minutes deal with administrative and disciplinary matters. Still appears there more than once, yet they make no mention of his infamous walk in the woods. They tell another story, however, one that surprises, especially coming from this shy, quiet, inner-directed young man who later wrote that he got in trouble for playing "pranks."

These minutes reveal that Still was involved in a knifing incident near the end of his junior year. Apparently he never told anyone in his later family about it, and it is now known only through the faculty minutes. Two weeks before the recital of his own compositions (mentioned above) was to take place, Still came before the faculty in a disciplinary proceeding for "cutting with attempt to wound" a fellow student. It seems that, along with some other men, he had joined a group of women students in defiance of school rules as they walked from building to building between classes. Told to leave by a nearby male faculty member, they did, but not before a male student monitor, assigned the task of escorting the women, pushed Still off the sidewalk with unnecessary force. No one, including Still, disputed that after the second push Still drew a knife, or that he used it to cut the student monitor. In his own defense, Still pointed out that the student monitor was much larger than he. Several student witnesses, speaking in his support, agreed that he had acted in self-defense.

Other students were expelled by the faculty that day for seemingly far lesser, "moral" infractions, but Still was not. (The assumption always was that, if male and female students were together and unchaperoned, even for a moment, a "moral" infraction had occurred. If male students joined female students on the sidewalk, as Still and his friends had briefly done, there was a potential moral infraction. Knifing, even if little damage was inflicted, would now seem to be a far more serious matter.) Instead, the faculty suspended judgment for a week, an unusual step, then voted to censure Still and take away his social privileges for the few weeks left in the semester. (That action would have provided a reason for canceling the scheduled concert of his own compositions, but we have no way to know for certain.) Recognizing through their action that there was more to the story and that most likely the student monitor had a history of bullying, the faculty also adopted a new rule restricting student monitors' behavior.[5]

We can't know why Still was not expelled on the spot. We can guess that at least some of the faculty came to his defense because they recognized his unusual gifts, perhaps because they depended on his contribution to the music that would shortly accompany graduation ceremonies, or perhaps because they had seen other bullying episodes before this one. It is possible that the advocacy of Hallie Q. Brown, a longstanding, highly respected member of the faculty who was acquainted with Carrie through their common interests in teaching English and in the Negro women's club movement, swayed the faculty. The practice of bringing disciplinary issues before the full faculty was abandoned immediately after the knifing incident; thus, we can't follow Still's career at Wilberforce any farther. That is likely why there is no formal record about the "picnic in the woods" episode the following year.

The memory of the knifing adventure, seemingly so out of character for Still, doubtless convinced him that there would be no further sympathy from the faculty after his "walk in the woods" with Grace Bundy the following year. Whatever led him to walk away before graduation, leaving school without his diploma, definitively ended his mother's dreams that he would abandon his plans for a career in music and go to Oxford to study. In retrospect, the knifing incident became a challenge to the disciplinary status quo, an outcome that finds a later parallel of sorts in Still's subtle, often unrecognized use of blues elements in certain of his compositions.

Ready or not, Still was now launched on his postcollege career. He had managed to get a considerable practical music education at Wilberforce in spite of its unpromising musical stance. He learned how to play and write for several band instruments, he made arrangements for various ensembles, and he made some useful contacts that helped him in the lean period to follow. On the other hand, the lack of systematic training in music—most immediately the absence of violin lessons—made it that much harder to earn a living as a performer, as he was now forced to do.

We may safely infer that the formal African American post-Reconstruction perspective Still found at Wilberforce was quite different from what was offered at predominantly white universities such as Oberlin. He must have absorbed some of this along with his general disrespect for the school's strict parietal rules. (He was not a regular churchgoer afterward, but he never abandoned the Christian orientation of his youth, even when he developed a strong interest in spiritualism and numerology.) In the "Personal Notes," his resentment about the time he spent at Wilberforce is tied to the fact that staying there kept him away from the study of music. Nevertheless, the seat-of-the-pants experience of those years left him more determined than ever to become a musician.

Ohio on His Own

When Still left Wilberforce, he went first to nearby Columbus, where, as he reported much later, he began to find work as a professional musician. The "Personal Notes" are laconic about the start of this period:

> After this affair I left college and went to Columbus, Ohio to make my own way. Managed to get a job. Made six dollars per week. Finally got a job with an orchestra. Did very well while the job lasted. After that I had to go a little easy on the eating so that there would be enough to eat a little each day. Nevertheless, in the fall of that year (1915) I got married . . . I will say no more of the marriage other than to mention that my mother was sorely grieved because of it, and to mention the four kiddies of mine. . . .[6]

One of the people who helped him at first was Nimrod Allen, a 1910 Wilberforce graduate who had become executive secretary of the new Spring Street Branch of the YMCA. Verna Arvey's much later memoir, *In One Lifetime*, elaborates further:

> He felt cut off from his family; he felt that he had done very little to justify his mother's hopes for him . . .
>
> He was still more discouraged when Tom Howard heard him play the violin and reluctantly told him that he wasn't good enough for professional work. . . . Then Tom Howard heard him practicing the *William Tell Overture* on the oboe and gave him a job with an orchestra that played in Cleveland's Luna Park—at fifteen welcome dollars a week. Howard liked his cello playing too, and let him play that as well as oboe. Work soon became more plentiful and he saved all he could out of his salary. He went into the National Guard Band, played oboe and fiddle in various orchestras and joined a group of musicians then playing at the Athletic Club. All of this was done in Mr. Shepperson's cast-off dress suit, which had to be held in place with safety pins because it was so very much bigger than Still was . . .[7]

At least a dozen or more bands were active in Columbus between 1915–1920, but there is no way to tell which of them gave Still work. It is likely that the *American Suite* for orchestra, found in the archives of the Chicago Symphony Orchestra, where he had submitted it, dates from this period. (It was neither acknowledged nor performed.)

W. C. Handy and Oberlin

The "Personal Notes" don't mention that Still spent several months in 1916 working out of Memphis with W. C. Handy, "the father of the blues." Handy had already become enormously successful as a bandleader through his instrumental adaptations of rural African American blues. According to his autobiography, Handy kept several bands busy touring in the region, thus he had work to offer.

Piano part, "No Matter What You Do," Still's first published piece. Memphis: Pace & Handy, 1916. From the John Robichaux Collection, courtesy of Hogan Jazz Archive, Tulane University.

Moreover, Handy had known of the elder Still's ability as a musician through his earlier teaching stint at Alabama A&I. Still made arrangements for Handy's bands—a half-dozen were published by the Pace and Handy Music Publishing Company—and toured with him as well.

The exposure he gained to the indigenous music of the Delta region in those months was extremely important to him, proving invaluable as he sought to find his voice as a composer later on. The clearest statement of this influence—apart from the musical examples scattered through Still's oeuvre—is to be seen in the draft foreword that Still wrote at the conclusion of his 1930 sketch of his *Afro-American Symphony* (discussed in chapter 6). Blues-based melodies and formal structures proved a fruitful source of inspiration for Still over the long term.

In her 1939 biography of Still, Verna Arvey does not mention Still's period with Handy. Yet, in a 1967 interview, Still commented about his early stint with Handy and his grasp of the importance of "Negro" music:

> I didn't come in contact much with Negro music until I had become of age and had entered professional work. I had to go out and learn it. . . .
>
> I realized that the American Negro had made an unrecognized contribution of great value to American music, particularly . . . in the blues . . .
>
> Of course the blues were looked down upon, people looked over their noses at them, and they were considered to be connected with the brothels. But in the South, where I had gone around and listened to them at their source, I felt that there was something more in them than that. I felt that they represented the yearning of people who were reaching out for something that they'd been denied. . . . There is something pathetic in the blues, something you hope to get some day, and it looks like you're not going to get it, but yet you haven't given up. I felt that hope and sorrow in the blues, and I wanted to use that idiom, I wanted to dignify it through using it in major symphonic composition.[8]

When he was in his seventies, Still recalled some of the less attractive features of the job that pointed up the evils of segregation. By that time, there were calls for black separatism by younger African Americans. Remembering the rigid and destructive barriers of his youth and middle age, Still vigorously resisted any kind of segregation, whether voluntary or not. "Our traveling was done in Jim Crow cars, which were usually only half cars. They offered very little that was comfortable or desirable: cinders, smoke, unpleasant odors, and the feeling of humiliation, being compelled to pay first-class fare for third-rate accommodations. . . ."[9]

Still turned twenty-one in 1916, making him eligible to receive any remaining proceeds from the farm in Mississippi he had inherited as an infant, after his father's early death. In the fall, he left Handy and returned to Ohio. This time he was able to fulfill the ambition to which his mother had turned a deaf ear four years earlier; he enrolled as a music student at Oberlin. Oberlin's records show him enrolled in fall 1916 and again in 1917. Still's account in the "Personal Notes" is helpful for its discussion of ways and means:

> After a brief period I received a small amount of money that my father left me. With a por-
> tion of this I began studying at Oberlin. They were very kind to me there. Gave me work in
> the school assisting the janitor. This helped pay room rent. Dr. and Mrs. Stevens, colored
> people who kept and boarded some of the colored girls attending the school, allowed me
> to wait table at their place. This provided food. I also played in the moving picture house
> there on some nights. This brought in a little more. Of course the money I received was
> little. I often was unable to keep quite as neat as I would have liked to be. It's not easy to
> stretch a few worn articles of clothing. . . . While in Oberlin Prof. Lehmann, who taught me
> theory, seemed impressed with my work in the class. He asked me one day why I did not
> study composition. I told him that I did not have the money. . . . As a result Dr. Geo. Andrews
> was asked and consented to teach me composition free of charge.[10]

Still's copy of Lehmann's *Harmonic Analysis*, now at William Grant Still Music, is full of penciled-in notes, indicating that he was extremely interested in his theory course. Perhaps even more important to his development as a composer, orchestrator, and arranger, however, was Still's exposure to the concert life at Oberlin, which was more accessible than what was in Dayton, Columbus, or Cincinnati while he was at Wilberforce. The bulletins list numerous concerts by visiting virtuosi and visiting orchestras. For the 1916–17 season, the Philadelphia Orchestra and the New York, Chicago, and Cincinnati Symphonies all performed on campus, as did the Flonzaley Quartet and pianists Percy Grainger, Marian MacDowell, and Ossip Gabrilowitsch, among others. There were also numerous student performances. This was probably the first time that Still was able to hear full-sized symphony orchestras and their standard repertoire live with any frequency. (He had, of course, heard orchestral accompaniments as background on his stepfather's Victor Red Seal recordings, along with a variety of live performances by smaller theater orchestras.) Whether his work obligations allowed him to attend either performances or rehearsals and whether he could afford the price of admission remain questions, as does the question of whether he played in the Conservatory orchestra, which would have been substantially larger and more skilled than the one at Wilberforce.[11]

Still completed three semesters of part-time study at Oberlin. He left abruptly in the midst of the fourth, going to New York and enlisting in the U.S. Navy in early 1918. The U.S. had entered World War I, and there was a strong feeling among African Americans (eventually proved wrong) that volunteering for military service would be repaid by improved conditions at home. We don't know whether Still received a draft notice, but we do know he had played in a National Guard band in Ohio, and he sought to enlist in one of the black Army bands that were so well received in France. He served for eleven months as a mess attendant on a ship before being discharged. While he was stationed at Newport News, Virginia, he managed to pay a visit to Nathaniel Dett, whom he was destined to succeed as the most prominent African American composer of concert music at the time. (Dett, who was then teaching at the Hampton Institute, found him a bit uppity.) He also was able to go to the Metropolitan Opera at least once. For several months after his discharge, though, he floundered, as the "Personal Notes" show: "Worked then in a shipyard over in New Jersey. Working in winter. Had often to go in the double bottoms and bail out water. This did not agree with me."[12] After a quick trip to his wife's home in Kentucky, he returned to Ohio:

> No work in Columbus. Remained there looking and hoping. Was down to my last dollar. Really I had just one dollar left. That same night some musicians who lived in the same hotel where I stopped knocked on my door and told me that I could go to work with them the following night. The violinist who had been playing with them had gotten drunk and thrown them down on the job.
>
> Worked in Columbus for quite a while. Finally had some money ahead and returned to Oberlin. Stayed there for a period. The end of the session. Had written Handy about work in New York. He had been here about a couple of years then. He agreed to give me a job. (I had worked with him a few years before in Memphis. One summer only.) My wife went back to Kentucky and I came back here.[13]

His job in Columbus was in the Whispering Orchestra at the Kaiserhoff Hotel. For a time in spring 1919 he commuted to Oberlin on Wednesdays and Saturdays for lessons with Dr. Andrews, though he was not formally enrolled.

Still's experience as a working musician did not mean that he performed a steady diet of ragtime or early jazz in his Ohio years. Small bands such as those he played in, whether they were appearing at private parties, amusement parks, or other venues, were expected to read music and to play in several styles. Even for black musicians who often performed in very modest venues for very little money, "commercial" music had a broader meaning than we might now think from the now-customary idea that "popular" and "classical" music existed in totally separate aural and cultural compartments. Opera overtures, along with waltzes, marches, and two-steps, were an important part of their repertoire. A note in *The Freeman* confirms the varied repertoire of the time:

AMUSEMENTS AND ATHLETICS AT COLUMBUS, OHIO

Tom Howard's orchestra at the Athletic club will be cut down to three pieces, piano, flute and violin. . . . William Still, cello, will also close the season [on May 5]. . . . The orchestra made quite a hit here playing "William Tell," "Poet and Peasant," "Aida," "Raymonda," "Magic Flute," and a number of standard overtures.[14]

Playing in all-black groups did not limit Still's repertoire or his style nearly as much as early historians of jazz have liked to say. Nevertheless, his early path as a working musician was quite different from the more conservatory-oriented paths followed by many composers known for their concert music. Still's continuing practical performing experience, which was quite different from the more formal training paths followed by his white counterparts, sharpened his sensitivities and his skills as an arranger, leading to his unique approach to arranging and to orchestrating his own music. It influenced his own composition as well.

Much remains unknown about Still's Ohio period. One would like to know more about his work with W. C. Handy in particular. We do know that, by the time he left Ohio permanently for New York City, Still had prepared himself to take his place as one of the most successful—and most enigmatic—New Negro musicians of the Harlem Renaissance and, simultaneously and unexpectedly, as one of the most prominent of the young modernists of the 1920s.

4 | New York City

STILL'S FIRST WINTER in the New York area was just plain miserable. After his discharge from the Navy, he worked as a laborer, cleaning out the bottoms of ships. Presently, as he wrote to Forsythe later, ". . . Received a wire supposedly sent by my wife's father stating that she was dead. Left hurriedly only to find her alive and perfectly well when I arrived in Kentucky."[1] The telegram was a hoax, probably sent by Grace herself, but it got him away from the dead-end job. After a short stay in Kentucky, he found his way back to Ohio and resumed his lessons at Oberlin and his pickup work there until W. C. Handy, who had given him work earlier in Memphis, offered him a job in New York City.

We know that he was in New York in September, for he wrote to Giulio Gatti-Casazza, general director of the Metropolitan Opera, using Pace & Handy's return address: "I have recently completed an opera based upon Negro life in antebellum days. All of my hopes are centered upon its production. Will you assist me? I should be happy were you to consent to consider it. Very respectfully yours, Wm. G. Still." A few days later, he wrote again, this time in longhand:

I am sure that my first letter did not get into your hands as I have not yet received a reply. I realize that one in your position is kept very busy and that you have no time to waste upon

25

unknown persons. Were there other channels through which I could approach you I would resort to them . . .

There may be great possibilities in this work. Unless it is considered it will never be known whether or not it contains <u>any</u> merit . . .

Ten days after Still sent his first letter, he received a reply: ". . . it is not possible at the present time to examine your opera . . ."[2] The only known trace of this score, probably his third attempt at composing an opera, is in these two letters. (The first opera, or perhaps the first version of this one, was in high school and the second at Wilberforce; neither of these survives.) One is struck by Still's combination of naïveté, optimism, and self-confidence in this exchange. There would be at least one more attempt before the first opera for which there is a score.

It is difficult to follow Still's New York career as an arranger in much detail, especially in these early years. Like the other musicians with whom he worked, his jobs were often short-term. Much of his arranging work, especially at the start, was unsigned and remained anonymous, eventually known within the trade by typical touches like the novel instrumental combinations and woodwind licks in the breaks between phrases. Since most of his arrangements were sold outright or were considered part of his regular job, there are no royalty contracts. Any day-to-day appointment books or diaries he may have kept are also lost for the years before 1930. Even when his journals begin, the entries are often cryptic. Lists of arrangements in his sketchbooks give some hints, but most of the arrangements themselves were used a few times, never published or recorded, and remain unlocated today. Records from other sources are also either obscure or not yet thoroughly explored. Even for Broadway shows and nightclub revues, the instrumental parts were rarely kept after the show closed. The band simply walked away, leaving their parts on the music stands. If the conductor or someone else didn't choose to retrieve them, they were left for the janitors to discard.

For almost two years, Still's main job was as house arranger for the Pace & Handy Music Publishing Company in New York. He also played with Handy's band. The band traveled a fair bit, often in the South for as long as a month at a time, one reason why Grace was reluctant to join Still in New York. Harry Pace, Handy's business partner, worked with Still on several songs that the firm published, providing lyrics that Still set under the pseudonym "Willy S. Grant." More important were his (unsigned) arrangement of Handy's "St. Louis Blues," the first for band, and his (signed) version of the "Hesitating Blues."

Three months after the Pace & Handy company dissolved, Still landed a position as oboist in the pit orchestra for the new all-black musical *Shuffle Along*, whose principal arranger was old Broadway hand Will Vodery, already arranging

Shuffle Along orchestra, 1921. Still, holding his oboe, is fifth from the right. Note the unusual instrumentation. Photographs and Prints Division, Schomburg Center for Research in Black Culture, The New York Public Library, Astor, Lenox and Tilden Foundations. Used by permission.

for the Ziegfeld Follies and later the first African American arranger to work in Hollywood. Hall Johnson, who later achieved fame as director of the all-black Hall Johnson Choir and popularizer of spirituals, sat next to him in the pit. (Neither Johnson's viola nor Still's oboe were standard instruments for a pit orchestra.) *Shuffle Along* opened May 22, 1921, at a theater on 63rd Street and ran for more than a year, drawing large, racially mixed audiences, unusual for the time. After a decade-long hiatus following the enormously popular Williams and Walker collaborations, *Shuffle Along* restored the all-black musical as a viable genre on the New York stage. In the process, it created new opportunities for everyone associated with it.[3] In addition to Still and Johnson, "everyone" included Noble Sissle and Eubie Blake, Flournoy Miller and Aubrey Lyles, Caterina Jarboro, Florence Mills, and Josephine Baker. Vodery and Mills turned out to be especially important to Still.[4] Vodery, who had more arranging work than he could handle, gave

28

his surplus to Still, whose hand (and stamp) show up on some of the surviving arrangements. Vodery introduced Still to Don Voorhees, one of several white bandleaders who eventually gave him substantial opportunities.

After 504 performances, *Shuffle Along* closed in New York and traveled to Boston for what turned out to be a run of three months. Still went along and took Grace with him. Early in the run, he sought out composition lessons at the New England Conservatory. George Whitefield Chadwick, a well-established older composer who was by then the director of the Conservatory, took him on as a private student, refusing to take a fee for the lessons. Chadwick, Still later reported, guided him through an accelerated theory course and encouraged him

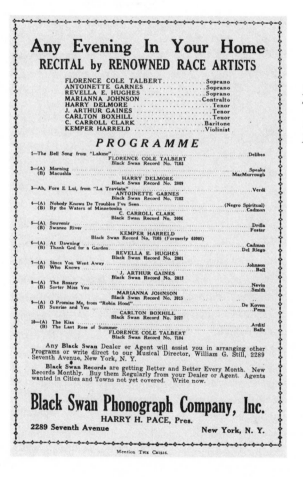

Black Swan ad in The Crisis, *February, 1923. Still is listed as Musical Director.*

to seek out a "characteristic" American idiom in his music. (Edgard Varèse, who taught Still later on, was less complimentary about Chadwick's teaching, but Still himself tended toward restraint in his written comments.)

Returning to New York, Still chose not to accompany *Shuffle Along* on its further travels. (Grace had disliked their stay in Boston. A prospective London run never materialized, probably a bone of contention between them.) Instead, he reconnected with Harry Pace (Handy's former partner), who by this time was running the Black Swan Recording Company, the first black-owned record label. Fletcher Henderson, Handy's recording director until then, had just left, and Still took his place.[5] There he composed, arranged, and supervised recordings. Ethel Waters recorded his pseudonymous "Memphis Man" and "Brown Baby"; the label also issued his "How I Got Dem Twilight Blues," "Love Me in Your Own Time," and "Go Get It," along with arrangements of the spirituals "Swing Low, Sweet Chariot" and "Steal Away," and, in a collaboration with Henderson, "Pretty Ways." There were more classical numbers, as the company's ads in *The Crisis* show. Black Swan's success with sales aimed at the African American market called the attention of the more established white companies to a demographic they had previously overlooked. By April 1924, the label had gone under in the face of their better-funded new competition, and Still was once more out of a job.[6]

While Still worked for Black Swan, he orchestrated James P. Johnson's music for Miller and Lyles's *Runnin' Wild*, starring Florence Mills (opened 1923). Still's earliest scrapbook includes an unsigned newspaper clipping with the comment "whoever arranged the music of James Johnson and Cecil Mack is something of a genius, we think." Like *Shuffle Along*, *Runnin' Wild* was a landmark for black music; by no coincidence, it was also the source of the national craze for that quintessential jazz dance, the Charleston. In addition to the band, the chorus electrified the audience by tapping and clapping out the complex rhythms of the new dance. It is likely that Still deserves a share of the credit for this success.

The contacts Still had made in the course of his work with Pace & Handy, with Sissle & Blake in *Shuffle Along*, and through Black Swan gave him new opportunities that extended through the decade. Vodery used him as assistant leader and sometime arranger and conductor at the Plantation Casino for an after-hours show featuring Florence Mills after she left *Shuffle Along*. Still followed that up with arrangements for *Dixie to Broadway* (1924), another (although somewhat lesser) success that involved Will Vodery and Florence Mills. Two other shows that he worked on at about the same time for Luckey Roberts, *Creole Follies* and *Struttin' Time*, flopped before they reached Broadway. He also made arrangements for prominent performers such as Sophie Tucker (in *Earl Carroll's Vani-*

Florence Mills, in
Shuffle Along, *1921.*
Still orchestrated for
Mills in several later
shows, including Runnin'
Wild *and* Dixie to
Broadway. *Photograph:*
White Studio, Museum
of the City of New York.

ties of 1924), whom he later singled out as a white performer who gave him an important opportunity, and various performers at the Plantation Casino, where he eventually succeeded Vodery as director. He played in a band with LeRoy Smith as well. By early 1925, he was already recognized by the principal *New York Times* classical music critic as "orchestrator of much of the music for negro revues and other theatrical attractions."[7]

Getting His Concert Career Under Way

Late in 1921, an art song, "Good Night," was sung in public by Revella Hughes, a well-known soprano who had also had a role in *Shuffle Along*, in a concert room on 138th Street, with Still's Ohio friend William Service Bell at the piano. Still also played oboe in the Harlem Orchestra at this period. The group began its concerts with music from the standard light classical literature of overtures and movements of symphonies from the European concert repertoire. Then, pausing for an intermission while the chairs were moved back and the rugs rolled up, they played for dancing. At least for a while, there was an audience for concert music offered by black performers in black-friendly venues, but this middle-class, relatively genteel practice was always marginal. (Neither African American musicians nor black audience members in any numbers were to be found at the Philharmonic's concerts.) As was the case even for all-white symphony orchestras in all but the largest cities, the Harlem Orchestra never had an audience large enough to support its performers, nor did it find patrons willing to cover its deficits, as the white orchestras did. Possibly Still's *Three Negro Dances* was written with this group in mind, but it is doubtful that this orchestra survived long enough to read it.

These performances, for black audiences, made friends for Still and gave him a chance to perform some concert repertoire, but they did not represent the entree he needed into the larger, overwhelmingly white world of concert music. The breakthrough came while he was working at Black Swan. Edgard Varèse, a French-born composer and iconoclastic musical innovator, was attempting to make a place for avant-garde music in New York. Wishing to include minorities in his quest, he wrote to Black Swan in search of promising students. (In this he was following an example set earlier by the Czech composer Antonin Dvořák, who had taught in New York for several years in the 1890s.) Rather by accident, as the family story goes, the letter fell into Still's hands, and so began two years of study, his longest period with any composition teacher. Varèse encouraged him to experiment with both form and content, and set him to study modernist scores such as Stravinsky's *Petrouchka*. More importantly, he encouraged Still to find his own way without imposing his own stylistic ideas on his student. In an often-quoted letter, he referred to Still's "lyrical nature, typical of his race." He added, "I handle him with care, not wishing that he should lose these qualities . . ."[8] Still admired Varèse greatly, finding both his teaching and his friendship valuable, even though he later distanced himself from his teacher's style of composing.

Varèse's support extended beyond the lessons that were squeezed in among Still's irregular but demanding commercial responsibilities. He opened doors to the world of concert performance by programming Still's music on concerts given by the new International Composers Guild at prestigious Aeolian Hall, where they were reviewed by New York's major music critics. At these concerts he met and heard some of the white modernist composers who were his contemporaries and, in this arena, his colleagues and competitors. Even more important, he met the conductors who would continue to perform his symphonic music over the coming decades, particularly Howard Hanson in Rochester, Eugene Goossens in

Cincinnati, and Leopold Stokowski in Philadelphia. His formal manners and his taste for elegant dress masked his shyness and admitted stage fright in this new, unfamiliar spotlight.

Although his commercial and concert careers often appear, especially in hindsight, to have taken place in separate, almost watertight compartments, the individual who was pursuing them was remarkably single-minded. Carlton Moss, a writer who later collaborated with Still, recollected just how focused Still was about his work:

> The only time I saw him was at the dinner table at the YMCA in Harlem, which was the only really decent place to eat. He would sit there, and he had this habit of tapping his foot. He never talked about anything else but that music. Later on I always felt that I was just an interlude. That I never talked to him about this lynching, or this problem, or what the NAACP was doing. I just listened to his loyalty to his music, and I got the impression that when he left me, wherever he went, he'd sit down and mess with that music. . . . He was very attractive, but he was always off, in another world.[9]

Negotiating his dual careers required just such persistence, though it came at a price. His constant preoccupation, combined with the irregular hours and the occasional travel required of him, probably contributed to the family miseries that were a part of life in his New York years. Nevertheless, he was determined to support his family and provide a stable, secure family life, as his mother and grandmother had done for him.

Still managed to compose several works, harbingers of his later achievement, in this period of study. Some will be discussed briefly in this chapter; several other instrumental works will be discussed in more detail in chapter 6. *From the Land of Dreams* was completed in 1924 and performed once, in February 1925, on a concert of avant-garde music sponsored by Varèse's International Composers Guild. Afterward, Still withdrew it and never offered it for performance again. (Although he did not destroy the score, it is not available for performance.) Its reception brought home the peculiar problems he faced as a black composer of concert music and helped precipitate an aesthetic crisis that he only gradually and partially resolved. Made up of three short movements, it is written for a small orchestra that included single woodwinds, strings, and three female voices "used instrumentally" (i.e., singing "ah" rather than a text) and used as another section of the orchestra, like the strings and woodwinds, rather than as soloists. Still's program notes refer to "the flimsiness of dreams" and "the borders of both the realms of fancy and of reality." The title, *From the Land of Dreams*, is most likely a reference to Still's longstanding interest in mysticism, occultism, dreams, and visions, "isms" that were then in vogue among his white contemporaries as well.

The dreams of his title seem to refer to the subconscious imaginings of older, forgotten cultures and lives, a major theme of theosophy. The voices, high, inchoate, singing in very close harmony and moving rapidly, can be heard as just such "flimsy" utterances. The piece employs modernist-sounding dissonance, advocated by theosophists like Dane Rudhyar (and tentatively accepted by some audiences) as mystically expressive. It lacks any clearly understandable references to music commonly thought of at the time as "black," although the dominant theme, articulated first by the oboe, might be heard in another context as a blues lick.

Audience reaction to *From the Land of Dreams* was puzzled, as was often the case for avant-garde music, but polite. The critics were generally not sympathetic to the idea that persistent dissonance had a special, mystical expressiveness, especially when it came from an African American who often worked uptown. Writing in the *New York Times*, principal critic Olin Downes thundered, "Is Mr. Still unaware that the cheapest melody in the revues he has orchestrated has more reality and inspiration in it than the curious noises he has manufactured?"[10] Still had, it seems, written music that did not fit the white critic's view of what music a man of color ought to be composing.

African American critic Alain Locke also took notice of *From the Land of Dreams* in his essay "The Negro Spirituals" in his 1925 *The New Negro*. After asking "why something vitally new has not already been contributed by Negro folk song to modern choral and orchestral musical development," Locke speculates, "Up to the present, the resources of Negro music have been tentatively exploited in only one direction at a time,—melodically here, rhythmically there, harmonically in a third direction. . . ." He posits that the western melodic tradition, the oratorio tradition, and most important the "traditional choiring of the orchestra" have "stood against the opening up and development of the Negro and the African idioms in the orchestral forms." He then names *From the Land of Dreams* as one of three "experimental tappings . . . into the rich veins of this new musical ore."[11] Locke's perception of Still as drawing on a rich non-European tradition went unremarked in Still's notes and utterly unrecognized in the generally white concert music establishment for which Still had written.

To be fair, Downes hadn't thought much of Varèse's works when they had been performed on earlier ICG concerts, either. Yet the racist slant of his (and other critics') criticism of *From the Land of Dreams* and his other works posed a problem and a challenge for Still, one that was not likely to go away. He could not simply compose as himself, allowing his cultural background to speak for itself, because his audience was unwilling to recognize anything in his cultural background but the clearest possible references to the spirituals or to the stereotype-laden "revues" he was orchestrating for a living ("jazz" was still a dirty word in many quarters; considering that, Downes's criticism was relatively restrained). If his racial difference was always going to affect the way his music was heard, then it had to become a conscious consideration for him as well. Something of an aesthetic crisis ensued. What should the music he composed be about? How best to communicate with the paying concert audience, which was largely white? These questions, always in the background, now came to the fore.

Still's period of study with Varèse was a major breakthrough, into a different world from that of nightclubs, pit orchestras, and commercial arranging. It started him, at least tentatively, on his career as a concert composer. As the reception of *From the Land of Dreams* forcefully reminded him, this career had different expectations and different casts of characters from his life as a working musician and arranger; it reinforces the differences between them of class and caste, as well as of musical style and genre, that in the 1920s were pushing the worlds of concert and popular music farther apart. Along with the breakthrough, he had to consider the racial issues raised by his intrusion into the highly specialized world of modernist concert music. Like it or not, he was going to be viewed by the mostly white audiences that attended such performances not just as another "serious" composer, but very specifically as an Afro-American composer of concert music. How were they to hear his visible otherness? Still clearly wanted to explore new musical territory and express his ideas with integrity, whatever the audience or venue. He found himself in a unique balancing act, one that often sought a centrist path that was not always understood from either direction.

While he considered his long-term aesthetic options, Still decided on his next project, one that would be performed on another Guild concert in Aeolian Hall. What he settled on as his reply to the critics was a kind of cosmic joke. He recruited his friend Florence Mills, whose songs he had orchestrated for the hit show *Dixie to Broadway* and at the Plantation, to be his soloist. *Levee Land*, characterized as a "Humorous Suite," was a set of four songs accompanied by an ensemble of clarinets, saxophone, violins, banjo, piano, and drums. The title made an explicit reference to American black culture, and the songs were relatively uncomplicated, although they were set against dissonant instrumental accompaniments, unusual enough so that learning the songs was something of a struggle for his soloist. The subtitle strongly suggests that with *Levee Land*, Still incorporated his own tricksterlike, cosmic humor in a response to his critics that was both "humorous" on its surface and deadly serious in its meaning for Still. The critics were marginally happier, and the full house was captivated by Mills's appearance. In his own way Still had succeeded in bringing Broadway to Aeolian

Hall, as Gershwin had done with his *Rhapsody in Blue* two years earlier. It remained for him to move beyond this lighthearted response to Downes's critique and to find his own aesthetic path.

The music notebook and the theme book he started during his study with Varèse bristle with melodic ideas. Some of them were intended for an opera, even though he didn't yet have a librettist or a storyline. And, there is a version of the large symphonic suite that eventually became his virtually unknown masterpiece, *Africa* (discussed in the next chapter). Thus began what he later called his "racial" period, a time of striking creative productivity. He would not stick to settings of spirituals, as other African American composers had done; he would also, for the most part, avoid the polite "symphonic jazz" of white musicians like George Gershwin and Paul Whiteman. In addition, he would avoid the more outrageous experiments in dissonance of the white modernists, for they carried the danger of subverting the Afro-American identity he now embraced. Following this reasoning, he abandoned his stunningly original *From the Land of Dreams*.

What emerged from such moments of reflection was a unique amalgam, a reconciliation of his commercial experience with his early conditioning about contributing to the race, along with his religious conviction. *Darker America*, a tone poem for orchestra, represents this synthesis. Still intended it to describe the "serious side" of the American Negro, "the triumph of a people over their sorrows through fervent prayer."[12] Themes representing sorrow, hope, prayer, and so on, are treated successively and together in a sectional form suggestive of an overture for a theatrical production, but in a quieter, euphonious mood. This tone poem brought him two awards, both received in 1928. The Harmon awards were conceived in the late 1920s as a way to recognize and reward achievement by African Americans in several areas; Still's was specifically for *Darker America*, which had its first performance in late 1926. As a result of a performance in Rochester the following year, the score was published by C. C. Birchard & Company—a signal mark of success in the world of concert music. Its early impact on the black critic Harold Bruce Forsythe, of whom more later, resulted in Forsythe's groundbreaking essay on Still, "A Study in Contradictions."[13] Ironically, Still himself later rejected this work as immature.

Grace

As all this was going on, Still was struggling in his family life. I write with a certain reluctance about Still's first marriage, to fellow Wilberforce student Grace Bundy.

Except for one recent interview and a few short letters, all of the reports now available have come through the formal divorce papers, filed in 1938, or through Verna Arvey, Still's second wife, like Grace a writer. It is easy to imagine a strong desire on both their parts to bury that part of his past. Whatever the reason, Still's journals and datebooks from the years of his first marriage, which might well shed more light on both his personal and professional life, are lost.

Grace is scarcely visible in the record while Still was in Ohio, for she spent most of her time in the early years of the marriage with her own family, near Danville, Kentucky. A formal photograph, taken in New York, shows a handsome, rather light-skinned, well-coifed individual. (Curiously, no snapshots of the couple or of a family group with children or grandparents are in the public record.) She came to New York only in 1921, after her husband had been there for two years. Reports are that the marriage was difficult and tumultuous from the start. Yet by the time Still moved to New York to take up his new job with Handy, they were parents to two children; eventually there would be two more. Except for Still's expressed fondness for his children, no positive statement about this marriage survives.

In New York, the couple worked at cross-purposes. Still's income was irregular through most of his New York years, especially at the start. His post-Wilberforce experiences still fresh in his mind, he was far more conservative about spending than she was. She chose places to live that required longer-than-necessary commutes and payments he could not cover. Later on he wrote of her bad decisions, such as buying a house they could not afford (they lost their investment in a foreclosure) and, several times, writing large checks on his account without telling him. My guess is, she thought he was aloof and preoccupied with his music, leading her to become ever more resentful; he was on the road a lot, was preoccupied to the point of obsession with his music, and probably didn't always pay enough attention to what was going on at home. As time went on, things seemed to get worse rather than better; indeed, it is hard to understand why they stayed together as long as they did. When we reach the period for which his journals survive (1930), there are frequent references to "conditions" at home that must have been well-nigh intolerable for both. We have hints that neither one was comfortable with the other's family, a contributing factor in a culture where extended family connections remained important. Early on, they had collaborated on one song ("No Matter What You Do," text unlocated, see page 20). At some point, probably encouraged by the performances his concert works were getting, they would begin working together on an opera, very likely on an African topic. It is possible that the failure of that effort was a contributing factor in their continuing malaise.

Still relied on personal religious conviction in order to live with Grace's vagaries. He kept a notebook that he later typed up neatly, entitling it "Praise Prayer, Truth and Testimony."[14] Some entries are dated as early as 1925. In it, he uses biblical language to describe the visions that reinforced his determination to continue in his chosen career and accept the burdens his marriage imposed:

Let not my tongue question God's will. . . .

Let not my voice be raised in protest 'gainst the judgement of One who makes the greatest adversities blessings unto them who love Him and keep His commandments; Who looks beyond the morrow even unto the end of this world. . . .

O, darkness, can there be no light? . . .

Despair, art thou supreme? . . .

He also addressed other temptations, though without naming them:

He who indulges to excess in worldly pleasures suffers not only loss of physical strength, but also blunts the edge of his conscience. . . .

'Tis the first breach in the wall of conscience that requires the greatest effort in the making. . . .

Repression of evil tendencies bespeaks not their absence. . . .

We simply have no way to know whether the sexual transgressions seemingly referred to here were committed by one or both of them.

Opportunity

Still was playing with LeRoy Smith in Atlantic City in the summer of 1926 when he got a cable from conductor Don Voorhees: "Put In Your Notice Immediately So That You Will Be Back Here No Later Than The Twenty Sixth Sooner If Possible Let Me Know If OK." Voorhees started paying him $100 a week as an arranger, a good salary at the time. At that point, Still was able to give up playing in public and devote himself to making music by putting notes on paper, sometimes in the form of arrangements done for a regular salary, and sometimes in the form of his own compositions.

5 | Making His Mark

> It's impossible to estimate the extent
> of his anonymous contributions to the
> lighter music of America.
>
> —Sigmund Spaeth (1948)

STILL'S NEW JOB WITH Don Voorhees brought stability and opportunity as well as a certain prestige. Voorhees (1903–89) was, like Still, a crossover musician. He was a conductor who had taken advantage of opportunities to ply his trade on Broadway and in radio rather than in symphony or opera, where Americans were rarely considered for conducting jobs. He is now mainly remembered for his long-running *Bell Telephone Hour*, one of the few radio shows that made the transition to television successfully, lasting into the 1960s. Still was on his payroll for two and a half years. Through Voorhees, Still found himself orchestrating several editions of *Earl Carroll's Vanities* (a series of revue-type shows that ran from 1923 to 1930) and one of J. P. McEvoy's *Americana* (probably 1928), as well as *Africana*, a show featuring Ethel Waters. Very likely he contributed to the effects in the *Vanities of 1928* that drew this comment from the *Times*'s drama critic: "stung by the jazzy lash of Don Voorhees and his squealing band, the music sweeps like a breaking wave." In 1928, too, he orchestrated the very successful musical *Rain or Shine*, starring Ethel Waters, one of the blues singers who had appeared on the Black Swan label.

Beyond the shows and recordings that Still worked on with Voorhees, there were experiments with radio, for Voorhees's orchestra was featured in ten hours of broadcasting per week over station WOR for a year starting in September

1927. Moreover, Still was in on developments that resulted from the introduction of electric microphones, which made a huge difference in broadcast technology as well as recording. (The electrically powered mike could pick up much more color and dynamic variety than could the older mechanical ones.) Voorhees was open to Still's occasional experiments, audible on some of the surviving recordings, with unusual soloistic ideas for the musicians. The experience he got with Voorhees was valuable in another way, for it led to his next several jobs, where he could develop his ideas further. In addition to these cutting-edge opportunities, Still was able to take advantage of the vogue for black entertainers by organizing orchestras for private engagements on several occasions.

In later years, Still was quiet about his work as an arranger and orchestrator on Broadway and in radio, in favor of his concert career. Critical opinion about "serious" music was based on a kind of social Darwinism, shared by a substantial portion of the concert audience. Popular music, regardless of its creators' race, was "merely" instinctive, lacking emotional depth or (especially) an intellectual dimension; composers of popular songs were thought to be even less likely to produce anything suitable to the concert hall than were, for example, women of any class or race. At the same time, concert music and commercial music were growing farther apart in the public consciousness. Even so successful a composer of popular songs as George Gershwin found it difficult to move from the popular to the serious side. Gershwin's example made it very clear that too close an identification with the "popular" was likely to interfere with a concert composer's career. His race made this an even larger issue for Still. African Americans who worked in the field of popular music and musical theater recognized that the sharp distinction between "classical" and "popular" carried negative cultural implications for them. Still's reticence about this aspect of his career stems, at least in part, from the very unequal values placed by the culture on his different kinds of work in music. Despite his later reluctance to advertise it, the evidence shows Still to have become as active and arguably as influential an arranger (though never as well paid) as Don Redman or Ferde Grofé, both now much better known as creative arrangers in the same years.

Still's commercial work provided him with a kind of experience significantly different from that of most other American composers of concert music who emerged in the 1920s. Many of the Caucasian composers of concert music who were his contemporaries avoided the "popular" route. They had access to patrons who contributed to their support, sometimes over long periods; others relied on their family's resources to launch their careers. Still others supported themselves through teaching, a path Still never wanted to pursue. In a society that did not reward nonwhite workers—including professionals—as well as white ones, he had to find his own financial support. Yet he benefitted from those opportunities, unusual as they were, using them to shape his unique and expressive style.

Still and Concert Music

The year 1926 turned out to be a big one for Still. His new job with Voorhees roughly coincided with the performances of his music (*From the Land of Dreams* in 1925; *Levee Land* and *Darker America* in 1926) at the International Composers Guild concerts that brought him to the attention of the concert music establishment. At last he had enough arranging work so that he could put aside his oboe, giving him more composing time. Beyond that, he received what was probably his first commission for a piece of concert music in late April or early May. It came from dancer Ruth Page, supported by Adolph Bolm and Chicago Allied Arts, to set a story from the island of Martinique. Its central figure was La Guiablesse, an evil spirit who, in the guise of a beautiful woman, lured men to their death. His letter thanking Page for the commission gives an idea of his manner of address as well as his concerns for the commission:

> May 6, 1926
>
> Dear Mrs. [Ruth Page] Fisher:
>
> First I must offer an apology for using the typewriter and explain my reason for doing so. Strange to say, in writing anything other than music I become so nervous that I lose control of the pen which results in altogether illegible script.
>
> Though I have not yet completed reading the book I have gained much valuable information therefrom. The descriptions of native customs, La Guiablesse, The Calinda, Bele and the drums are of the greatest value.
>
> Upon first reading your story I was favorably impressed with it as it offered me the opportunity to write that type of music which I know best and love—music of the primitive, elemental sort. As I have read and reread it since, my interest has grown until the story seems to have become a part of me.
>
> It is my custom, before beginning work on anything, to pray for Divine guidance which I have done in this case. Now strange themes, so in keeping with the character of your story, come to me. I have every reason to believe that you will not be disappointed in the music and that the ballet will be a success.
>
> Sincerely yours,
>
> [signed] William Grant Still[1]

The formal courtesy and the religious reverence with which he approached his task as a composer were characteristic of the man's public persona and his written expression, likewise the somewhat stilted style and, contrary to his statement, his very clear handwriting. His interest in "music of the primitive, elemental sort" was especially characteristic of this, his racial period, and it remained an essential aspect of his musical approach. *La Guiablesse* remained unfinished for several years, as did *Sahdji*, a second ballet project based on an African story that did not come to fruition right away but was ultimately even more successful. With each, he struggled to reconcile the "primitive" imperative with his sophisticated technical understanding. Eventually the role of La Guiablesse would be danced by the long-lived, versatile Katherine Dunham, who resurfaces in Still's later, Hollywood years.[2]

Paul Whiteman in Los Angeles

In 1929, the white bandleader Paul Whiteman sought an African American arranger for his unique, enormously popular orchestra. Like a symphony orchestra, it featured a large violin section; also a large woodwind section that could, with some strategic doublings, supply a saxophone quartet. Both woodwinds and brasses were comfortable—and sometimes, later on, individually very successful—with jazz styles. It was this orchestra that had introduced George Gershwin's *Rhapsody in Blue* five years earlier, confirming the popularity of what came to be called "symphonic jazz," and probably stimulating Still to begin his series of "race" compositions. Still, whom Whiteman judged the most successful among those he auditioned, was signed as the band departed for Hollywood in May 1929 to make their movie *The King of Jazz*.

Still had a fruitful relationship with Voorhees, but Whiteman offered more promising opportunities even though the salary was no different. Whiteman and his orchestra had a much higher public profile, and higher pay was promised in future contracts. (This was a promise Whiteman was unable to keep, for, as it turned out, he could not match Voorhees's professional longevity.) Whiteman's orchestra was larger than those used in theatrical productions, offering the possibility of creating new sounds. Moreover, Whiteman's orchestra wasn't confined to a theater pit; it was the main attraction. There was also the chance that Whiteman would be in a position to perform some of Still's own compositions. (*The Black Man Dances*, for solo piano and orchestra, a work that strongly deserves revival, was commissioned by Whiteman later on, as was *A Deserted Plantation*. So was "Land of Superstition," the third movement of *Africa*.) The wide gap between Still's commercial work and his concert music was not working to Still's advantage. This move provided an important new opportunity, one that might function to bring the two styles of music closer together. Added to that was Still's alienation from Grace, which had clearly grown. His mother's death two years earlier severed the last ties he had felt with his extended family in Little Rock. Grace, who remained hopeful that they would eventually go abroad, refused to go with him to Los Angeles.

It was through Whiteman, then, that Still came to spend a year in Los Angeles, an experience that presently changed his life, both personally and professionally. Still's contract with Whiteman was not connected to the movie, *The King of Jazz*, that took him there. Rather, he was hired to make three arrangements weekly, about thirty pages of score, for Whiteman's radio show, the *Old Gold Hour*, broadcast from Los Angeles while Whiteman and his band made the movie. Still considered that rather substantial amount a light load. "Since I am a pretty fast worker, that gave me a great deal of time to myself." He used it in ways that had not been open to him at home in Queens.

Still rented a cabin in one of Los Angeles's black neighborhoods (still relatively small) from his cousin Charles Lawrence, himself a musician and bandleader. One of his neighbors was Harold Bruce Forsythe, a younger musician and a writer as well, whom he had met in New York several years earlier (about whom more in a later chapter). Forsythe had already become an enthusiastic advocate of Still's music. Although there is little direct acknowledgment of his influence, Forsythe was something of a catalyst for Still, stimulating him as he completed his major "racial" period works. The tendency to overstatement visible in Forsythe's writing balanced Still's inclination to pointed brevity. It is easy to imagine Forsythe talking enthusiastically and Still quietly addressing, and eventually moving away from, most of Forsythe's ideas.

Compositions from c. 1930–32

On his return to New York in May, 1930, Still used what turned out to be seven months of unemployment to take care of some important unfinished business, that is, his concert music. Later, he marked this as the period of his artistic maturity, and for good reason. For at least some of that time, remembering the absence from family tensions that had been part of his first Los Angeles experience, he rented a small apartment in Harlem where he could work with minimal interruption. His first project was a major revision of the orchestral suite *Africa*, an extremely important work discussed in the next chapter in more detail. A version with reduced scoring had already been played in New York by the Georges Barrère Little Symphony, but Still now wished to revise the full score for a performance scheduled for late October in Rochester, New York. (The conductor in Rochester was Howard Hanson, director of the Eastman School of Music. Hanson was to prove a strong supporter over the next decade.) *Africa* has had a strange history. Still assigned the rights to it and several other works to publisher Jack Robbins when he left New York in 1934. Robbins retained it long after he had returned the other works. As late as 1947, Still tried, unsuccessfully, to recover control over *Africa*. By then there were many other works in his catalog and other issues to struggle with. At this writing, publication of the score is, at long last, in process.

The other two of these works have fared far better. (Both found friendlier publishers; J. Fischer & Brother was particularly supportive. The death of its owner in the early 1940s was a serious loss for Still's career.) The gestation period for the ballet *Sahdji* had been almost as long as that for *Africa*. The ballet, largely composed in Los Angeles, needed polishing. As soon as he finished *Sahdji*, he sent it on to Howard Hanson, who promptly scheduled it for production the follow-

Left to right: Howard Hanson, Director, Eastman School of Music, who conducted several of Still's works; Gene Buck, composer and president of the American Society of Composers, Authors, and Conductors (ASCAP); Still; composer and critic Deems Taylor. Photograph: Cosmo-Sileo. Courtesy of Ruth T. Watanabe Special Collections, Sibley Music Library, Eastman School of Music, University of Rochester.

ing May (1931). *Sahdji* was revived several times in Rochester in the course of the 1930s and eventually recorded by Hanson. The *Afro-American Symphony*, by contrast with *Africa* and *Sahdji*, was created in a single burst of activity in the last two months of 1930, beginning shortly before the premiere of *Africa*, and just after the opening of Gershwin's hit musical *Girl Crazy*. It too is discussed in the next chapter. Like *Sahdji*, the *Afro-American Symphony* would also be premiered in Rochester, conducted by Hanson.

Even while he was working on those three major works, Still was taking on a lot of freelance work and looking for a steady job. Presently he was hired by the (white) singer-songwriter Willard Robison to orchestrate his radio show, the *Deep River Hour*, which was broadcast on WOR three days a week. Robison had a very light, high baritone voice; he sang old favorites (including many by W. C. Handy) with a southern, somewhat rural feel. Still was able to extract an unusually rich variety of instrumental colors from Robison's small radio orchestra, supporting Robison's light voice without overwhelming it. Insiders knew he was the program's very creative arranger (and occasionally composer), though his name was never mentioned over the air. Presently, at the request of the musicians in the orchestra, he became its conductor. The distinctive and widely admired style of arranging Still developed in the course of this apprenticeship is audible in a few surviving aluminum recordings.[3]

Enter Opera: Exit Grace

In 1933, the *Deep River Hour*, which had never found a commercial sponsor, came to an end. Still once again had to rely on freelance work to meet his continuing expenses. The Great Depression was still gathering force, hitting the music and theater businesses particularly hard. This was not all bad for Still, at least for a while. He had been thinking about composing opera for some years. Earlier, while he was working for Voorhees, he had begun a collaboration with Grace on *Rashana*, to be based on a novel that Grace was developing. Together they had worked out an outline for a libretto, setting up a series of dramatic scenes that would tell the story through music. They recruited the newly successful Harlem Renaissance poet Countee Cullen to turn the outline into verse. Only a few musical ideas in Still's sketchbook and a handful of letters from Grace to Cullen survive from this attempted collaboration. Grace's letters to Cullen brusquely reject whatever suggestions Cullen offered concerning the outline.[4] (Cullen's letters to the Stills, like Grace's novel and the outline of the opera, remain unlocated.) In any case, Cullen was soon distracted by his other interests and never returned to the project. If Still tried to pursue it, no evidence survives.

During the run of the *Deep River Hour*, Grace left, taking their children to Toronto, Canada. She had sorely wanted to emigrate to France, using Still's considerable savings from his work in Los Angeles to get started. She had written in December 1929 to Countee Cullen, with whom she was still corresponding over *Rashana*, "I am eagerly awaiting the summer to make my first visit to France. I feel quite as you do about letting the children grow up there and as soon as possible after this proposed visit plan to begin looking about for permanent quarters for the family." Still had wavered about this possibility. In a moment of frustration more than a year later, a few days after he had completed the *Afro-American Symphony*, he wrote to Irving Schwerké, an American critic living in Paris:

> It is unfortunate for a man of color who is ambitious to live in America. True . . . there are many splendid people here; broad-minded, unselfish; judging a man from the standpoint of his worth rather than his color . . . But there is a preponderance of those who are exactly the opposite. And the views of the former must, of necessity, conform more or less to those of the latter.
>
> I have never felt this so keenly as in the past few months. Friends who would lend me a helping hand, who would make it possible for me to make a living for my family, are unable to do anything because of those who are opposed to placing a colored man in any position of prominence. That is stating it mildly . . .
>
> Unless there is a change soon I will be forced to abandon my aspirations and look to other means of gaining a livelihood or to go where such conditions do not exist.[5]

He could not have known that within a few months his brand-new *Afro-American Symphony* would ensure his place in the history books.

Still had resisted going abroad when Florence Mills had gone to Paris and London with the Plantation orchestra, and he resisted again when his year in Los Angeles with Whiteman left him with money in the bank. The reasons can only be guessed. Grace had been reluctant to come to New York; once in New York she had been reluctant to travel to Boston with *Shuffle Along*. He was uncertain whether he could support his family abroad without reverting to the life of a performer, something he clearly resisted, and there were no prosperous relatives or patrons to rely on as guarantors. He had learned the hard way not to trust Grace's handling of their finances.

It is not entirely clear whether Grace's departure was meant to be a final separation. One story is that Grace had gone in search of a job that evaporated once she reached Toronto. Grace is conspicuous by her absence from Still's only surviving comment on their departure, written a few months later in the "Personal Notes": "Gee, but I love those kids . . . I never fully knew how greatly I was wrapped up in them until I was separated from them." She returned to New York with the children at some point, but it is unlikely that Still lived with them again. A letter to Still, sent after his move to Los Angeles, implies that she expected him to return to New York and resume the relationship. This was apparently not a reasonable expectation from his point of view.

After her children left home, Grace Bundy lived out her life secluded in a darkened brownstone in the Jamaica area of Queens, the Long Island neighborhood she had chosen against her husband's wishes, surrounded, as a grandson reports, by her books and her literary manuscripts. William Bundy Still, their son, made a modest name for himself in early television and sought occasionally to renew the connection with his father, even visiting him in California once, around 1960. In his letters to his father, he claimed that Grace was manipulative and less than honest, and also granted that his sisters disagreed with him. The younger Still's difficulties with his own life suggests a regrettable pattern of anger, failures of communication, and the abrupt, often permanent cutting of family ties that appears across several generations of Still's family.[6] When Still remarried later on, he was profoundly appreciative of his second wife's loyalty and her zealous support, likely a result of having sorely missed those qualities in Grace.

Parted from his contentious family, Still contemplated another opera project (actually two operas), this time working with his Los Angeles friend Harold Bruce Forsythe. He applied for a Guggenheim fellowship for support while he worked on an opera, a much larger project than anything he had previously tackled. He did not get the fellowship on the first try, in 1933, but in 1934 he did. He lost little time in leaving New York. Instead of heading to Europe as Grace had wanted, he pointed his car westward, with the intention of making the move a permanent one.

6 | Still's
Instrumental Music

STILL'S EARLY EXPOSURE as a concert composer brought him more opportunities and commissions, mainly for orchestral works. Varied though they are, the resulting compositions share some common elements. He began each of them by working with short melodic ideas, which he wrote down in his "theme books" as they came to him; then, treating them with increasing skill as building blocks, he worked out his extended forms. As part of the building process, he often drew on structural or harmonic elements common to the blues, though these references are often not immediately obvious. He often drew his basic inspiration for a work—which themes to use, and how to put them together—from visual or literary images. Thus word clues—sometimes quite understated—from Still's program notes or his scores often amplify the expressive ideas one hears in his music. This discussion draws heavily on hints from those clues.

The verbal cues begin with Still's choices of titles; abstractions like "symphony" or "suite" are always elaborated. Many are suggestive of African American life or of Still's pan-African interests: *Darker America, Africa, Sahdji, La Guiablesse, Afro-American Symphony, A Deserted Plantation, Levee Land, Song of a New Race, From the Black Belt, Ebon Chronicle, The Black Man Dances, And They Lynched Him on a Tree, For the Colored Soldiers Who Died for Democracy, Lenox Avenue,* and more. Other titles have a more general focus: *From the Land of Dreams, Dismal Swamp,*

Festive Overture, Plain-Chant for America, From the Journal of a Wanderer, Song of a City, and *Poem for Orchestra,* to name a few. These and other titles are applied to many different forms: symphonies (five of them), one-movement tone poems, multi-movement suites for orchestra, ballet music, works specifically for radio, pieces that include chorus or vocal solos, and piano and chamber music. Here I will describe just two of these works, the *Afro-American Symphony* and *Africa.* The first of these is now his best-known composition; the second a scarcely known masterpiece. It is important to remember that these are just the tip of the iceberg in terms of Still's output. They serve here as guideposts toward enriching the reader's understanding of Still's remarkable musical contributions. Because a CD could not accompany this book, readers are urged to seek recordings of these works, especially the ones discussed in any detail, from one of the download services available on the World Wide Web, such as Rhapsody.com or emusic.com.

Afro-American Symphony

In addition to the variety of Still's titles, additional verbal cues appear in his program notes and sometimes in his scores, suggesting more about the music. The best-known example of this is the *Afro-American Symphony,* composed in late 1930. One of the descriptions Still provided as a program note for this work has this symphony portraying the "sons of the soil, . . . who have not responded completely to the transforming effect of progress." The symphony may be taken as a record of that transformation as he saw it, progressing from "Longing" and "Sorrow" through "Humor" to "Aspiration," the four subtitles he suggested for its four movements. A blues-type theme is his basic building block for all four movements. Blues were still considered to be disreputable in 1930 because of their "lowly origin"; thus, he felt the need to defend this choice for its true reflection of "the anguish of human hearts" and for another reason as well. In his sketchbook, he made his argument:

> I harbor no delusions as to the triviality of Blues, the secular folk music of the American Negro, despite their lowly origin and the homely sentiment of their texts. The pathos of their melodic content bespeaks the anguish of human hearts and belies the banality of their lyrics. *What is more, they, unlike many Spirituals, do not exhibit the influence of Caucasian music.* [emphasis added]
>
> The Afro-American Symphony, as its title implies, is representative of the American Negro. In it I have placed stress on a motif in Blues idiom. It is employed originally as the principal theme of the first movement. It appears also in various forms in the succeeding movements, where I have sought to present it in a characteristic (style) manner.[1]

In addition to the usual tempo words (for example, *adagio*, meaning "slowly") and the English-language affect (mood-suggesting) words found at the beginning of each movement, an excerpt from a poem by Paul Laurence Dunbar precedes each of its four movements. The poems Still selected suggest his expressive intent; they also hint at the novel structural practices he devised as he went about composing this, his first symphony. For the first movement, he cites Dunbar's "Longing":

> All my life long twell de night has pas'
> Let de wo'k come ez it will,
> So dat I fin' you, my honey, at last,
> Somewhaih des ovah de hill.

The movement is a loose set of variations on the blues tune introduced at the beginning by the English horn and then the muted trumpet. This is quite different from the long-established notion of a symphonic first movement as encompassing the "development" and resolution of contrasting ideas that were still expected from a piece carrying the label "symphony." The difference is not only melodic, for it carries through in the harmonic stasis that is a characteristic of blues melodies. In the context of a symphony, this was a novel practice for 1930, unexpected and generally unrecognized by white critics. The second movement carries forward the blues idea, this time prefaced by lines from this African American poet with a far darker expression of sorrow and despair:

> It's moughty tiahsome layin' 'roun'
> Dis sorrer-laden erfly groun',
> An' oftentimes I thinks, thinks I,
> 'T would be a sweet t'ing des to die,
> An go 'long home.

The couplet attached to the third movement, a scherzo (i.e., a musical joke) barely three minutes long, is, because of its position in the poem from which it is taken, far less straightforward in its meaning.

> An' we'll shout ouah halleluyahs,
> On dat mighty reck'nin' day

This is the next-to-last couplet of a longish poem by Dunbar titled "An Antebellum Sermon," in which a slave preacher meditates on the biblical story of Moses leading the Israelites out of captivity, all the while exhorting his listeners not to get any ideas about finding freedom from their own bondage. He slips, though, with the couplet Still quotes, leading to this conclusion:

> When we're reco'nised ez citiz'—
> Hun un! Chillun, let us pray!

Still did not include this last couplet, nor did he identify the poem; thus his listeners could only know his intent if they were already familiar with Dunbar's poem.

The narrative found within this movement confirms the implication of the quoted couplet as it appeared in the (not quoted) context of the whole poem. In fact, it constitutes one of Still's little-understood cosmic jokes. After a brisk introduction, the French horn quotes George Gershwin's recent hit tune, "I Got Rhythm," loud and clear. (Conductors, not knowing why it is there, sometimes try to suppress this quotation. There is a good deal of evidence that Still believed Gershwin had picked up the melodic and rhythmic ideas in that tune from Still's preperformance improvisations in the orchestra pit during the run of *Shuffle Along* a decade earlier. The idea can't be confirmed definitively, but it is not beyond the realm of possibility. In any case, Still deliberately made that melodic quotation very prominent, and did not change it when he had a chance.) This tune quickly breaks up and disappears in favor of the cheery cakewalklike melody that dominates the movement. Three times this melody is interrupted by the trombones with a fanfarelike declamation, each time a little different, each time longer and more insistent. I read this movement as the symphony's very serious turning point, for all its lighthearted brevity. Beginning by quoting a white composer's representation of a black composer's improvisation, it ends with a black composer taking over the job of representing his own musical practice. Each of the trombone fanfare/responses sounds more like a personal emancipation declaration. Thank you very much, Still's trombones seem to say, now we'll speak for ourselves, using our own style to answer and elaborate as we will.

Movement four, following this slightly disguised revolutionary statement, reflects aspiration, quoting the first stanza of what is now Dunbar's best-known poem, leaving behind the broad dialect of the earlier quotations:

Be proud, my Race, in mind and soul,
Thy name is writ on Glory's scroll
In characters of fire.
High 'mid the clouds of Fame's bright sky,
Thy banner's blazoned folds now fly,
And truth shall lift them higher.

Its long, slow opening section—another "irregularity" for a symphony—expresses the dignity of Dunbar's poem; the fast-moving concluding half of the movement conceals some elements of the original blues melody, along with an homage to the whole idea of "American" concert music—including concert music based on the folk music of its humblest citizens.[2]

Still's originality in using a blues melody to construct a symphony is worth noting, not only because "originality" is highly valued in composers, but because, at the time the symphony was written, it represented his position as an African American creative artist intending to demolish the old stereotypes. By contrast, white composers tended to focus their attention on the rhythmic novelties they could absorb from jazz or blues rather than on their inherent expressive potential, as Still was doing here. Consider, for example, what the differently situated Aaron Copland wrote, just a few years later, with surprising condescension, about jazz:

> What interested composers, however, was not so much the spirit, whatever it symbolized, as the more technical side of jazz—the rhythm, melody, harmony, timbre through which that spirit was expressed. . . .
> By far the most potent influence on the technical side was that of rhythm.[3]

Copland, the son of Russian Jewish immigrants, was engaged with his own issues. He soon lost interest in this music because of its "severe limitations." Still, sensitized by his own experience as a black man in a highly segregated America, found dramatic new expressive possibilities in those very elements. This symphony constitutes just one of the ways Still found to define his personal African American identity through the medium of concert music.

Africa

The *Afro-American Symphony* was composed in about ten weeks and performed within months; it has subsequently been performed hundreds of times and recorded several more. The history of *Africa*, a large-scale suite for orchestra and one of Still's most important works, is entirely different. Beyond a few performances of a version for piano that tends to mask its basic structural elements and cannot reveal its dramatic use of orchestra color, almost nothing more of this work had been heard until a first orchestral recording was released in 2005. Yet, after its first performance by a full orchestra in the fall of 1930, Still wrote in his journal, "*Africa* was a sensation." Given that his private assessments of his own work were consistently restrained, and given the revelation of this recording, one must conclude that its obscurity is, to say the least, not deserved. In fact, *Africa* is a long-lost masterpiece.

To judge from his sketchbook and surviving versions of the score, Still may have begun work on *Africa* as early as 1924, though 1927 is more likely, despite the earlier date later written on one version. While he was writing out what became the next-to-last version of this work, in 1932, he commented, "I have never worked on any composition as long as I have worked on *Africa*. This period of work has extended over five years. . . . I believe *Africa* will endure."[4] Since the most recent version of the score is dated 1935, we may conclude that the work's gestation period turned out to be even longer than five years.

Africa is Still's meditation on the idea of a place that few black Americans had visited, but which had indelibly—and indefinably—marked their cultural identity. As the land of their origin, from which their forebears had been forcibly removed, the African continent was enveloped in a cloud of mythology. Yet the dream/idea of Africa as an idealized land of lost opportunity played a key role in the awakening of the 1920s that is called the Harlem Renaissance or the New Negro movement. Still, who lived and worked in New York in the years of the Renaissance, attempted in this work to reflect on and respond to these American imaginings about Africa. Marcus Garvey's meteoric career drew on—and illustrates—the resonance of what was still called the "Dark Continent" for American blacks, especially the working class, in the early 1920s.[5] It is highly unlikely that the nonpolitical Still was ever a member of Garvey's movement, but he could not have missed its presence in Harlem. It is easy to see in *Africa* Still's struggle to address the same cultural issue.

Still's basic idea for the work is found in a program note he included in the "Personal Notes": "An American Negro has formed a concept of the land of his ancestors based largely on its folklore, and influenced by his contact with American civilization. He beholds in his mind's eye not the Africa of reality but an Africa mirrored in fancy, and radiantly ideal." He organized this concept into three movements, respectively titled "Land of Romance," "Land of Peace," and "Land of Superstition." Each is a distinct idea, represented differently in the music.

"Land of Romance," the longest movement at nearly thirteen minutes, starts quietly and builds to its climax, then dies away in a shorter diminuendo. Its themes are dominated by the melodic interval of a whole step. Three tom-toms answer each other softly by way of introduction. A single flute then enters with a lyrical, improvisatory-sounding solo that emphasizes a rising step, with the accent on the lower note. The melody is taken up by other instruments, leading to a much more assertive contrasting theme, almost a syncopated fanfare, first stated by the horns in four-note chords. This theme is more rhythmic than the opening melody. It, too, springs from the interval of a second, but this time the emphasis is on the descending step. This idea continues to build, leading to the movement's climactic moment, the thematic revelation of Still's "radiantly ideal." This dignified, triumphant theme turns out to spring from the second theme, stated half as fast and losing its syncopated feel. From there, the climax dissipates, with brief references to the original flute theme before it dies out.

The "Land of Romance" movement exists in several versions that show three layers of revision over the years, offering a rare opportunity to examine Still's changing aesthetic stance in the process. The earliest sketch (from 1924 or 1926) shows only the opening and closing sections, with the modal feel of the opening soliloquy (given to the oboe rather than the flute) and the whole-tone, somewhat dissonant usages of the following, more fragmented elements, and is charactistic of his "ultra-modern" phase. (Empty space is left for a long mid-section in this version.) The unabashedly tonal middle section, with its striking French horn quartet, was added later (1928 or 1929); it suggests Still's "negroid" usages of the later 1920s. Even after these basic elements of theme and instrumental color were in place, in fact after *Africa*'s 1930 premiere, Still radically revised the architecture of this movement, from a symmetrical arch form (A-B-C-B-A, with C as the keystone of the temporal "arch") to its present form, with the dying-away greatly shortened (A-B-C-a). This, the final version, suggests a Golden Mean–like proportional structure for the movement rather than the earlier symmetry.

The other two movements exist only in single versions. "Land of Peace" is a sustained, muted legato movement that consciously avoids the tumultuous dynamic contrasts in the two outer movements. Its lyricism is emphasized by its three-part form, in which the third section is a literal repetition of the first, in the manner of a da capo aria. Conductors who were impatient with its deliberate peacefulness sometimes cut this movement, a loss for their listeners.

"Land of Superstition," the concluding movement, moves more quickly and builds aggressively to another climax. Its theme, which is treated almost like an ostinato (a short theme that "obstinately" returns, supplying a framework), is introduced by the basses. Its most prominent feature is a rising tritone (also called a diminished fifth or augmented fourth), left unresolved, making for a deliberately ungainly effect even though it is balanced by a chromatic descent in the second half of the phrase. (Early European theorists called the tritone *diabolus in musica*, the devil in music. In traditional European harmonic usage it had to be carefully resolved, yielding a strong sense of arrival. As in this movement, modernist composers of Still's time went to some lengths to use the tritone in ways that avoided the obvious tonal resolution that it had long implied.) It is likely that Still used this interval, with its "devilish" implications, to represent the "superstition" of his movement title. Still made an arrangement of "Land of Superstition" for Paul

Still, photograph probably taken for Paris performance of Africa, *autographed to Irving Schwerké. Music Division, The New York Public Library for the Performing Arts, Astor, Lenox and Tilden Foundations. Used by permission.*

Whiteman's orchestra; Whiteman played it, independently of the other movements, several times in the 1930s.

Still was clearly not interested in a literal, accurate representation of Africa in this work. Yet *Africa* displays a kind of integrity and authenticity that would be unimaginable in a more direct representation of a distant culture. Because it represents something far more immediate—an idealized vision that informed his sensibilities and those of his fellow citizens—*Africa* becomes a powerful, positive statement of American black identity; by extension, it becomes a quintessentially anti-colonialist American work. Thus the aesthetic behind this work was far ahead of its time even though it uses the harmonic and melodic language of its own day. At the urging of critic Irving Schwerké, *Africa* was performed in France in 1933. Because it was caught in a contretemps with a publisher, *Africa* went unheard after Still himself conducted one movement in the Hollywood Bowl in the summer of 1936. We will never know whether it would have become as well known to concert audiences of his time as his other large works. Clearly, though, it is a work for our own time.

7 | Los Angeles, 1934–

IN HIS OHIO YEARS, Still had wondered whether he would ever be able to break into the world of music as a composer. Now, as he drove westward in the spring of 1934, Still could contemplate what he had achieved. Over his fifteen years in New York he had built a solid reputation, first as a performer and then as an arranger. He had emerged as a promising composer of concert music. A substantial list of compositions and a series of prestigious performances had won him a position of prominence among the younger American composers of "serious" music. In the process of all this, he had managed to support himself and his family (from which he was now separated) in a creditable manner. His move to Los Angeles marks the start of another fifteen-year run of mature achievement and increasing recognition as a composer.

By his choice of Los Angeles over New York or Paris as his permanent residence, Still was dramatizing a radical new approach for a composer who wanted opera and symphony to be his primary focus. If composers of "serious" music went to southern California at all, it was usually on a temporary basis, to make money in Hollywood. Still himself had done this when he had followed Whiteman there in 1929–30. It is true that Still chose Los Angeles because commercial work might be available after the opera was completed and his fellowship money used up, but that was quite different from going there specifically to compose an opera, with no immediate commercial plans at all. In effect, he was expatriating himself from the Harlem Renaissance as surely as if he had gone abroad.

The move carried serious risks. He was distancing himself from the national center for concert music and opera and from the (mainly white) world of modernist composers, though not from the new technologies of commercial music. His comments suggest that he hoped to escape the ever-widening split between the worlds of commercial and concert music, with all their implicit racial and class associations, finding instead a path he could follow with artistic integrity toward a music that used the sonic resources of concert music and still had wide audience appeal. He called this his "universal" approach, one that broadened out from the specifically "racial" without abandoning it. Unfortunately, choosing Los Angeles as his base was sometimes seen, especially by white modernist commentators, as *prima facie* evidence that he had given up his "serious" goals and "gone commercial" rather than as a brave new statement.

As for the implications of his choices vis-á-vis the pressing political and social issues of the 1930s—a decade of unprecedented depression and dislocation—he clearly was seeking a perspective that would allow him personal space as well as maximum room for his creative work. That would (maybe) be easier in Los Angeles, where he might literally distance himself from the political and cultural pressures that were unavoidably associated with musical modernism. Besides that, he wanted to get away from the personal issues around his marriage. His immediate, business reason for leaving New York, however, was much more straightforward. He had an award in hand, intended to support him for a year while he undertook to compose an opera. This was a new, large project unlikely to bring financial rewards even in the long term. For this, he needed to be away from his arranging clients and close to his librettist.

The variety and abundance of Still's work in those early Los Angeles years seems almost kaleidoscopic. Even so, there was never much financial prosperity. Most of his income came from fellowships (two from the Guggenheim Foundation, one from the Rosenwald Foundation), commissions for new works, and fees for performances of existing works, normally collected through ASCAP. Yet he was, in many ways, living his dream, composing full-time, something that few American composers of concert music, regardless of color, have ever been able to do for long. He was even able to turn down arranging jobs early on. Only much later, in the 1950s did the lack of commercial work and a falling-off of interest in his orchestral music create a serious financial problem.

Still seems to have had no regrets for his decision. He had clearly found the

Los Angeles area to his liking during his earlier, very productive stay. The city was quieter, more spread out, its urban tempo more relaxed than New York's. Surface trolley lines, buses, and cars were an aesthetic improvement over the long subway commutes that had been his lot. Because of its distance from the old South and the relative expense of getting there, Los Angeles in the 1930s had a relatively small black population, which lived in modest but not overcrowded middle-class neighborhoods (often alongside the more sizeable Mexican population), well served by a public school system with a strong music program. Literacy—including musical literacy—was very high among the minority populations. Race-based violence against African Americans was relatively low, partly because the black population was relatively small in numbers, and partly for an uglier reason. Other minorities (Chinese and Mexican especially) had historically borne the brunt of white racial animosity in California.

Much of this would change drastically after 1940, when the newly established war industries brought a huge influx of black workers who found themselves crowded into the old neighborhoods, drawing resentment from the older residents and sometimes violent reactions from the white population. By that time, however, Still had put down his roots and was irrevocably committed to his Los Angeles lifestyle. He was so committed to Los Angeles that, even before the social changes wrought by America's entry into World War II became clear, he turned down a 1941 invitation from Alain Locke to join the faculty of Howard University in Washington, D.C. (Still did not seek out a teaching appointment or composition students in Los Angeles, either, though later in his life he mentored younger composers and often made school appearances.)

Billy and Verna and Harold

The welcoming committee that greeted Still after his cross-country drive in May, 1934, consisted mainly of Harold Bruce Forsythe and Verna Arvey. Forsythe's presence was Still's immediate reason for going to Los Angeles, although Arvey eventually became more important for him.

Forsythe and Arvey had been friends since their student days at Manual Arts High School. Each was a pianist, a writer, and a composer. Forsythe had met Still in the course of an otherwise unhappy year of study in New York in 1927. Deeply involved in the Los Angeles version of the New Negro movement, he had contributed to the short-lived magazine *Flash* and written a novel (*Masks*, also called *Frailest Leaves*, unpublished) that appears to be heavily autobiographical, along with several essays. His music and his writings contrast abruptly in style and content;

the songs are notable for their slightly old-fashioned, restrained European flavor, while his writings show an absorption with African myth and an extravagant literary style. He was deeply impressed, therefore, by Still's use of the European-based medium of concert music to express a vision of the African American experience that was both profound and feisty, something he had not found a way to do. That explains the gist of his essay, "A Study in Contradictions" (c. 1932, unpublished until 2000) on Still and his work.[1] In it, he labeled Still "the most revolutionary Negro composer ever heard of." His essay was inspired by an examination of only three of Still's already numerous scores: *From the Land of Dreams, Levee Land,* and *Darker America.* His insights are the more remarkable because he reached them without seeing the scores to *Africa, Sahdji,* or the *Afro-American Symphony.* Even more surprising, Forsythe's essay was the first detailed examination by an African American critic of Still's work, and the only one for several more decades. The fact that it remained unpublished for so long, and that he was unable to write about more of Still's music, has left a gap in the reception history of Still's music. Almost as an aside, Forsythe's "A Study in Contradictions" contains one of the few physical descriptions we have of Still in this period: "handsome in a languid Latin manner, inclined to portliness, and with eyes that glow with an unholy and unhealthy light when working, or when a beautiful woman interests him." A lengthier essay on *Sahdji* followed. As Still arrived, Forsythe had already produced a draft libretto for *Blue Steel,* the opera Still was preparing to compose.

Arvey, who had chosen further private piano study over college (at least partly for financial reasons), eked out a living by accompanying dancers, supplemented by frequent contributions to *The American Dancer* and, later on, *The Etude.*[2] From her high school days, she made a journalistic specialty of interviews with prominent figures in the worlds of music, dance, theater, and film. (A lengthy historical work on the dance, published in 1941, was developed largely using a questionnaire widely circulated to composers and dancers.) The daughter of nonobservant Russian Jews who had grown up in Chicago and come to Los Angeles as young adults, she had been raised in Los Angeles and had often served as the pianist in the theosophist church to which her parents belonged. She first met Still in 1930, when Forsythe asked her to read Still's draft scores on the piano. Soon after he arrived in 1934, she was volunteering to help with Still's considerable business correspondence, writing articles and publicity for him, and performing the piano music he wrote for her. She abandoned her own attempts at composing after observing Still's systematic, intense work style as he went about his opera project.

By the time the opera was completed, a triangle had formed among Still, Forsythe, and Arvey, in which Forsythe became the loser. Plagued by increasing deafness and recurrent illness, Forsythe was eventually forced to abandon music, a wrenching emotional loss as well as the end of his livelihood as a pianist. Before he foundered in a sea of anger, depression, and alcohol induced by his devastating health problems, he had been a good friend to Still, writing about his music with insight and passion and supplying one libretto and scenarios for two ballets. (*The Sorcerer* exists as a short piano score; *Central Avenue* was eventually revised for a radio commission, becoming *Lenox Avenue*.) Presently he retrained as a nursery-man, married, and fathered two sons, one of whom placed his papers and music at the Huntington Library, but he remained isolated from his early friendships.

Arvey and Still became a couple only with considerable hesitation. The fact that Still would at long last have to seek a divorce from Grace was one obstacle. (The black press gave his colorful 1938 divorce filing front-page treatment, an unwelcome indication of his prominence.[3]) Racially mixed marriages were forbidden by California law, which meant that the couple would cross the border to Tijuana for the wedding. The social consequences of a mixed marriage, however, could not be as easily circumvented as could either of these two rather substantial barriers. Los Angeles was a relatively open place in terms of race relations, but there were sharp limitations.

Probably Arvey was unaware of just how risky the mixed marriage was, even as their friendship grew. Anti-Semitism was common in Los Angeles, but Arvey nevertheless had access to much of the extensive music club culture that sustained numerous local musicians. The race discrimination they now faced—from both directions—was another matter. Her family had once objected when she had included Forsythe among her circle of friends, but there had been a reconciliation, or at least an adjustment. Now she was unprepared for—and, for that reason, more hurt by—the open hostility directed toward her by people of color. On at least one occasion, a lecture-recital on Still's music in Salt Lake City, Arvey had attempted to "pass" as African American, a tactic that, given her own Semitic features and coloring, had little chance of success. Still's friend John Gray reluctantly admitted to receiving hate mail after he had programmed Arvey to appear on a concert with an African American pianist. Even Florence Cole-Talbert, whose Black Swan recordings had been supervised by Still years earlier, wrote to Still, gently chiding her old friend: "I am afraid the white folks will take you away from us now that you have arrived—if they have not already done so (smiles). I know they gave you your opportunity to progress but after all you belong to us— n'est-ce pas?"[4] The long-term result of all this was that the new couple tended to avoid situations in which they might be vulnerable—that is, mixing with the general public.

In personal terms, the marriage must be counted as successful. By creating a comfortable and quiet home and through her absolute loyalty, Arvey provided Still with the stability that had been missing from his first marriage. In addition, Arvey did her best to keep their family (two children) afloat financially, continuing to write and, for a time, perform. (Her earnings were always modest. Eventually her parents overcame their early reservations and helped out as they could.) Even before the marriage, she had become a strong advocate and defender of Still's interests as she saw them, and a fierce protector of his composing time and his privacy. Still was enormously appreciative; the couple's mutual admiration was often remarked on by their friends and visitors. In the rare instances when Verna allowed her sense of humor to show, it was often ironic and sharply edged. Still's sense of irony shows in his music (*Levee Land* and the Scherzo of the *Afro-American Symphony* are examples, dating from his pre-Verna years), and his playfulness is occasionally visible elsewhere, as in his letters to the African American dancer/ choreographer Katherine Dunham from the mid-1930s, though not in the surviving correspondence with Arvey.[5]

Their professional collaboration was less successful. In addition to the isolation that went with the racially mixed marriage, Verna's protectiveness and her apparent lack of graciousness were not always constructive, as will be seen. Nor did her literary gifts and sometimes narrow views rise to the level of his talent. Her discomfort with the culture of New York City and her political outspokenness had consequences as well. Still was grateful to her for managing his correspondence, but did not rein in her sometimes abrasive style. Finally, it was not long into the marriage before Still came to rely on her almost entirely for librettos to his operas and for song texts, thus limiting the range of literary materials available to him. True, he had struggled to find librettos earlier; on the other hand, early in his Los Angeles years he worked with others, especially Langston Hughes and Katherine Garrison Chapin, to good effect. But in confining himself to the products of Verna's pen, he limited himself unnecessarily.

There is little question that his first marriage had ranged from being an irritant (in its better moments) to being a source of near despair. (Verna later compared Grace to the destructive, mythical spirit-villain of the ballet *La Guiablesse*, danced by Katherine Dunham.) Though the outcome of his second marriage was very different, and their racial positions were not the same, Still's two wives had some things in common that are indirectly suggestive of Still's personality. Like his mother Carrie, both wives were strong-minded women. Also like Carrie, both were writers. (None of Grace's or Carrie's work is known to survive, however.) Still worked with both to create librettos. The opera project with Grace was never completed, while Verna systematically carried through, eventually producing librettos for six operas. Still relied initially on his wives to handle his business correspondence; Grace apparently proved unreliable in this regard, while he quickly came to trust Verna's work, sometimes to excess.

Composing Opera

Still brought almost fifteen years of direct experience with commercial musical theater to the composition of *Blue Steel*, his first surviving, completed opera. At last, he would be in charge of what happened onstage, and the decisions could be made on the basis of dramatic and musical requirements as he saw them, not as a producer or star might demand. (*Sahdji* and *La Guiablesse*, the two ballets that had already been produced, were left entirely to the choreographers to realize.) He relished the challenge, but he found it more difficult and time-consuming than he had imagined. In fact, he asked for and received a six-month extension of his fellowship from the Guggenheim Foundation in order to finish *Blue Steel*, even though he worked steadily and quickly.

Back in New York, Still had initially proposed two operas. One was to be set in Africa; "its music will, in as far as artistically possible, reflect the primitive and barbaric nature of the African savage." He started in, however, on one whose materials he knew much better: "the scene of the second opera is to be laid in the United States, and its musical idiom will be that of the American Negro." He had already begun working on *Blue Steel* when he arrived in Los Angeles in 1934. The plot was based on a short story by his friend Carlton Moss, who was just getting started as a writer for radio.[6] Its setting is an isolated community in a "mythical southern swamp." In its story, a city-slicker from outside woos the chief's daughter, leading to a voodoo scene and a climactic, terrifying chase.

Still began by developing a detailed dramatic outline for his setting. He intended his outline to present "roughly and concisely the gist of the lines which are to be given each character, and the stage directions." Forsythe dutifully supplied language on demand to suit the composer's specifications. After *Blue Steel* was finished in 1935, Forsythe agreed to write a libretto for a full-length "Sorcerer." *The Sorcerer* now exists only as a piano score and a scenario suitable for a ballet, much shorter than a full-length opera would have been. Apparently that is as far as either one got with the project.

Apart from a couple of preliminary readings of individual numbers, *Blue Steel* was never produced. That was not for want of trying. The Metropolitan Opera, the country's largest opera company, ignored it, as it did most American operas. American composers as diverse as Virgil Thomson, Gian-Carlo Menotti, and George Gershwin all produced their major operas on Broadway, basing their decisions on such issues as timeliness, control over the production, preferences for the intimacy of Broadway's smaller theaters, and the Met's history of poorly (as well as rarely) produced American novelties. For his part, Still wanted to make a major racial statement by having his opera produced in an opera house. *Blue Steel* was not to be the vehicle for this breakthrough, however. Still put it aside after his second opera, *Troubled Island*, was completed a few years later. To this day, *Blue Steel* has not been produced.

Prospering, Modestly

Still wrote to Jack Robbins, the publisher who agreed to handle his music when he left New York, that he would have no choice but to return to New York if he failed to find work after his fellowship ran out. After some worrisome moments, he was signed to a six-month contract with Columbia Pictures. (It is possible that Robbins, who had strong ties to Hollywood, helped get him that position; they had not yet had their falling out.) There, Still produced a series of "sketches for the catalog," short musical bits to be plugged into stock situations in the low-budget, grade B movies that were Columbia's main product. These showed up in various films for years, and sometimes even appeared as fillers on CBS television series. They were owned by Columbia, however, and he apparently received little or no royalties from them. His contract was not renewed, probably as the result of a prank that has the earmarks of one of his cosmic jokes.

Contrary to its usual practice of churning out the low-budget potboilers for which Still had provided fillers, Columbia undertook a blockbuster, *Lost Horizon*, while Still worked there. The studio hired a small army of orchestrators to expedite the project, then kept them all waiting around without explanation. In a quiet scene for which he had already composed serene music, Still penciled in a loud phrase of a song, "The Music Goes Round and Round," for the trumpet, expecting to erase it immediately after the first run-through. When it was played, everyone on the spot laughed—except, as several versions of the story go, the director, Frank Capra, whose opinion counted the most. Dmitri Tiomkin is credited for the music in the film, which is not considered one of Capra's best. Although a few small jobs came Still's way after that, it would be six long years before another studio contract came along.[7]

There were many other opportunities, though. He conducted the Philharmonic at the Hollywood Bowl, a first for an African American; he programmed

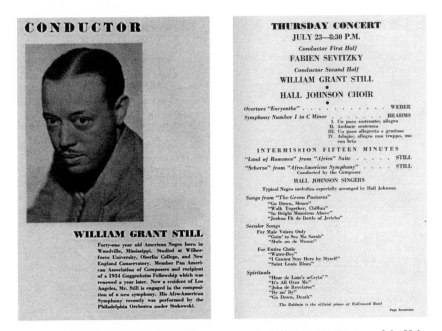

WILLIAM GRANT STILL

Forty-one year old American Negro born in Woodville, Mississippi. Studied at Wilberforce University, Oberlin College, and New England Conservatory. Member Pan American Association of Composers and recipient of a 1934 Guggenheim Fellowship which was renewed a year later. Now a resident of Los Angeles, Mr. Still is engaged in the composition of a new symphony. His Afro-American Symphony recently was performed by the Philadelphia Orchestra under Stokowski.

THURSDAY CONCERT

JULY 23—8:30 P.M.

Conductor First Half

FABIEN SEVITZKY

Conductor Second Half

WILLIAM GRANT STILL
•
HALL JOHNSON CHOIR

Overture "Euryanthe" . . . . WEBER
Symphony Number 1 in C Minor . . . . BRAHMS
    I. Un poco sostenuto; allegro
    II. Andante sostenuto
    III. Un poco allegretto e grazioso
    IV. Adagio; allegro non troppo, ma
    con brio

INTERMISSION FIFTEEN MINUTES

"Land of Romance" from "Africa" Suite . . . . . STILL
"Scherzo" from "Afro-American Symphony" . . . . STILL
    Conducted by the Composer

HALL JOHNSON SINGERS

Typical Negro melodies especially arranged by Hall Johnson

Songs from "The Green Pastures"
    "Go Down, Moses"
    "Walk Together, Chillun"
    "In Bright Mansions Above"
    "Joshua Fit de Battle of Jericho"
Secular Songs
   For Male Voices Only
    "Goin' to See Ma Sarah"
    "Mule on de Mount"
   For Entire Choir
    "Water-Boy"
    "I Cannot Stay Here by Myself"
    "Saint Louis Blues"
Spirituals
    "Hear de Lam's a-Cryin'"
    "It's All Over Me"
    "John de Revelator"
    "By an' By"
    "Go Down, Death"

The Baldwin is the official piano of Hollywood Bowl

Page Seventeen

Left: *Page from Hollywood Bowl program book, July 1936. Courtesy of the Hollywood Bowl Museum.* Right: *Page from Hollywood Bowl program book, July 1936, showing Still's part of the program. Apparently he suggested including Hall Johnson's chorus. Courtesy of the Hollywood Bowl Museum.*

excerpts from *Africa* and the *Afro-American Symphony* and shared his allotted time with his old friend Hall Johnson. He completed a second symphony, subtitled "Song of a New Race," which he saw as the completion of a trilogy following *Darker America* and the *Afro-American Symphony*. It was promptly performed by the Philadelphia Orchestra, under Leopold Stokowski.

Among other things, he received two contrasting, rather lucrative commissions that suggest the level of recognition he had achieved as well as the range of his abilities and interests. Still was one of six prominent composers of concert music to receive a commission for a work for radio orchestra from the CBS radio network. (The other five were Aaron Copland, Louis Gruenberg, Roy Harris, Walter Piston, and Howard Hanson.) Still had earlier begun a ballet on the theme of Central Avenue, the center of the black business and entertainment district in Los Angeles. Now, short of time, he withdrew *Central Avenue* from a performance he had promised to Howard Hanson and Rochester, NY, then revised and expanded it to produce *Lenox Avenue*. *Lenox Avenue* emerged as an orchestral suite made up of short, colorful movements descriptive of the diversity of Harlem's lively main street; the movements were connected with brief spoken narratives. Its heavily syncopated "Blues" movement for piano in particular became quite popular. After it was broadcast over a national hookup, *Lenox Avenue* was adapted as a ballet and performed in Los Angeles.

The other commission was for something that was eventually heard by hundreds of thousands of people. It came from the organizers of the 1939 New York World's Fair. Still composed *Song of a City* as the background music to be played as people walked through the Perisphere, an enormous white globe in which they could view a visionary model of tomorrow's world. The judges were reported in *Opportunity* to have "unanimously agreed that the author of *Lenox Avenue* and *From A Deserted Plantation* seemed to be most capable of giving musical expression to the mood and color of the theme exhibit." Of this he wrote to his friend Alain Locke, "It seems to me that this must be the first time, musically speaking, that a colored man has ever been asked to write something extremely important that does not necessarily have to be Negroid, and I must admit that I can't help being proud of the distinction."[8] He composed it in what he had already come to call his "universal style."

Still's most important work of direct racial protest came from the same period. In 1940 he was offered a poem by Katherine Garrison Chapin, wife of the United States Solicitor General, written in protest as a congressional filibuster threatened to defeat a much-needed federal antilynching law. *And They Lynched Him on a Tree* has an unusual form, developed to fit the semidramatic nature of the poem. A white chorus, a Negro chorus, a male narrator, a contralto soloist for the mother's blueslike lament that forms the work's middle section, and a symphony orchestra all are part of the work. (A decade later, this mixing of styles was dubbed "third stream.") Like many of Still's works from these years, it had a high-profile premiere, by the New York Philharmonic in their Lewisohn Stadium summer concerts. Two years later, it was broadcast over the NBC network, this time with Stokowski conducting. Reviews were positive, though some reviewers were bothered by the piece's atypical form.[9] (Black and/or female composers were commonly accused of inability to construct large musical forms, especially when their message, like this one, required unusual approaches.)

Somewhere along the way Still was dubbed "Dean of Afro-American Composers," a title that appeared regularly in program notes and on radio broadcasts starting in the late 1930s. The informal title honored the position of distinction he had achieved. At the same time, it set limits on how his achievements would be recognized, and at a point when he seemed to be shattering one barrier after another. What he always aspired to was to become "another American voice," using culture-specific resources when they were appropriate to whatever projects he chose to undertake. But "another American voice" was always understood as an *African* American voice, granted an often-varying but always-limiting range of expressive relevance for most white listeners.

Stormy Weather

In 1942, Twentieth-Century Fox approached Still to be music director for *Stormy Weather*, which would have an all-black cast, with the idea that his expertise with commercial music making would allow him to make a signal contribution to the movie. At the studio, he was quickly brought back to reality. ". . . I did not approve of Newman's ideas that in order to be authentic, Negro music had to be crude and Negro dancing had to be sexy. . . . those are the sort of misconceptions that . . . indirectly influence the lives of our thirteen million people. . . ."[10] Later, Arvey added, "Everything he did was thrown out . . . It was 'too polite' for Negro music. It was 'not erotic enough.' 'Negro bands didn't play that well in the Twenties,' he was told . . ."[11] Years later, Still gave this account of the incident (probably through Arvey):

> I was in on that because—as I was told when I was approached to be musical advisor—the plans were for a portion of the picture to have to do with some of the achievements of colored Americans in music. When I got there, I found out that was not so. It was all popular music, so there was very little for me to do. I just sat there in an office and twiddled my thumbs all day long. Finally [I] resigned.[12]

Still's resignation from the movie well before he could draw all of his promised salary was very public, thanks to news releases widely distributed by Arvey, especially to the black press. The family wondered whether Katherine Dunham, who had once had an eye for Still and was also hired to work on *Stormy Weather*, had a hand in his departure. (Anxieties generated by the mixed marriage seem to have surfaced here, but the volatile Dunham may indeed have played a role.) Whatever the reason, this was the last substantial commercial opportunity to come his way from the film studios, permanently cutting off one potentially important source of income. (He composed music for two wartime movies made by the Office of War Information: *The Negro Soldier* and *Tunisian Victory*, although his scores were not actually used in the films.) Not long after the *Stormy Weather* episode, Still wrote diplomatically, "I must confess that I don't know exactly where the line of demarcation comes: what is racial prejudice and what is inherent in the business

Katherine Dunham, who danced the title role of La Guiablesse *in Chicago and was part of the* Stormy Weather *production. Library of Congress, Prints & Photographs Division, Carl Van Vechten Collection (Reproduction Number LC-USZ62–93100 DLC).*

of film-making." Although he never wanted to make writing for the movies his first priority, a few more assignments would have eased the constant money worries he faced after his series of fellowships ran out in the early 1940s.

Publisher Jack Robbins had retained the rights to *Africa*, claiming that he would persuade the studios to use it in some way. Nothing came of this idea, however. Yet, at least for a time, Still's arranging skills remained in demand. Artie Shaw, big-band director and masterful clarinetist, contracted with him to provide him with the arrangements for a set of records that he had contracted but not yet made. An interview with the temperamental Shaw, published in *Music and Rhythm*, concluded, "Time will tell if Shaw, with his idealistic outlook, makes his mark in American music. American music—native music—is all he is interested in. His recent recording of William Grant Still's *The Blues* typifies what he considers to be the real American music—a music that will live. Artie Shaw wants to popularize that music. He wants Negro composers and musicians to realize something for their efforts. Artie Shaw is an unusual personality with unusual ideas."[13] Still received $441 for the set of arrangements, about fifty dollars apiece. One of them, "Frenesi," became a major hit, earning Shaw a very substantial profit, but no added bonus for Still. Such arranging assignments got much scarcer as the era of big bands slipped away. By 1950, Still was having a lot of trouble "realizing something" for his efforts.

8 | *Troubled Island*

OF ALL THE MUSIC Still composed, two large works have attracted the most attention from recent writers. One of them, the *Afro-American Symphony*, discussed in an earlier chapter, is now his best-known composition. Four different recordings are currently in print, and it is regularly found on concert programs and radio broadcasts, especially during Black History Month. A number of Still's earlier works were performed by symphony orchestras before the *Afro-American Symphony* appeared, but that is the one that was (and is) so widely performed that it must be considered the real barrier-breaker for Still as far as concert music is concerned.

The second work, paradoxically, is known far more by reputation than by its actual music. That is the second of his eight operas, *Troubled Island*, to a libretto by Langston Hughes. Produced in 1949 by the New York City Opera, *Troubled Island* was the first opera by a U.S.–born composer of any race to be produced by a major company, and the first by a black composer to be produced in the United States. Its production inaugurated what has become by now a long tradition by that company of producing new operas by American composers.[1] Yet *Troubled Island* remained the only opera by a black composer to be performed by that company until Anthony Davis's *X: The Life and Times of Malcolm X* appeared in 1986, almost four decades later.[2] There are now dozens of opera companies in

Langston Hughes, librettist for Troubled Island. *Library of Congress, Prints & Photographs Division, Carl Van Vechten Collection (Reproduction Number LC-USZ62–92598 DLC).*

the United States, but there were only three at the time, making this production an even more remarkable breakthrough.

If Still's career can be said to have had a single high point, this was it. Yet there was a downside that became evident soon enough. *Troubled Island* received its three scheduled performances, then faded into the (extensive) purgatory reserved for operas that do not enter the regular repertoire. The disparity between its initial reception—described in the Introduction—and its failure to achieve a wider hearing became a source of profound disappointment for Still and for his family, a disappointment that continues to reverberate among his descendants. Because the event proved so important to his career, this chapter takes up the history of the production in some detail. (That does not mean that others of Still's operas are not worth discussing and, more importantly, worth producing. They are.)

The path that culminated on that March evening covers a good many years. It began with poet Langston Hughes, who, as early as 1928, made his first sketches of a play recounting the tragic career of Haitian revolutionary hero Jean-Jacques Dessalines. A few years later, the resulting play, *Drums of Haiti*, was produced in Cleveland and Detroit. Hughes soon began to think of making it into a "singing play." Eventually he approached Still to compose the music.[3] This opportunity was a gift for Still, who had struggled to find librettists. He had turned to Grace for the story of *Rashana* and the young Countee Cullen for the lyrics; this project fell through for personal reasons on all sides. The less experienced Forsythe had made the libretto to *Blue Steel* from a short story by another friend, Carlton Moss. As it turned out, *Troubled Island* was the only one of Still's operas on which he worked with an established poet, one whose fame was as well established as his own. (Katherine Garrison Chapin approached him to set the poem that in 1940 became the cantata *And They Lynched Him on a Tree*. Soon after that, she provided the text that he set as *Plain-Chant for America*, which had many performances during World War II. After that, although he composed six more operas, he never again worked with any writer but Verna Arvey.[4]) Hughes's light and facile touch with words was important to the opera's shaping. More important, the combined reputations of Still and Hughes guaranteed their collaboration a high public profile, invaluable in achieving the actual production. Very possibly their public break just before the premiere may have assured its subsequent burial.

The Haitian revolution was powerfully attractive to both men as a theme. Arna Bontemps—another writer with whom Still once discussed a possible collaboration—put his finger on one of the reasons when he wrote to Hughes that *Drums of Haiti* "presents Negroes in a mood unfamiliar to usual stage productions."[5] An opera on blacks successfully freeing themselves from the oppression of slavery would constitute a major political statement, one very different from the works of white composers on stereotypical "black" topics (several such, all now better-known, are listed near the end of this chapter), and far more challenging to its audiences than the earlier black-composed musicals that played off the old minstrel/vaudeville stereotypes (by, for example, Will Marion Cook or Sissle and Blake). Other themes in the opera would challenge the predominantly white audiences as well; for example, the bitterness between the uneducated black field slaves and those who were racially mixed and literate; the massacre of the white population (which takes place offstage, between Acts I and II); and the portrayals of human emotions and aspirations that are presented as universal rather than stereotypically "Negro" qualities. The reality of singers of both races portraying blacks in serious historical situations on the operatic stage, with only marginal references to the traditions of "black" entertainments, would be a new one for almost everyone involved, including the cast, the audience, and the critics. (It is very likely that confusion over how to read those widely recognized references in this new context affected the opera's reception.)

When they could finally sit down together to work on the project in spring 1937 (before that, Still was busy with his Symphony no. 2 in G Minor, "Song of a New Race," and the *Lenox Avenue* commission), they came up with four sections for the opera. In the first act, the slaves gather secretly and Dessalines takes charge; the rebels agree that the mulatto slaves who have administered the plantations may join them despite their differences. After a ritual sacrifice, arms are distributed by Dessalines's wife, Azelia. The act ends with a rousing chorus as the former slaves go off to fight. Act II takes place several years later. Dessalines, now the emperor, embraces the trappings of a ruler but struggles to govern in the face of his own illiteracy, revealing himself as unable to make the transition from military to political leader. He is ridiculed and cheated by the educated, mixed-race advisors on whom he must rely. In the next scene his second, mixed-race young wife and his lead advisor plot against him; he departs to quell a rebellion by his own army. In the concluding act, Dessalines is murdered by his erstwhile followers, the plotters leave for Paris, and Dessalines's first wife, Azelia, returns to sing a lament over his body.

The evidence suggests that Still and Hughes came to an agreement on everything except—perhaps—the conclusion. After an intense six weeks together, Hughes went off to Madrid to write dispatches on the Spanish Civil War, leaving a tenth of the needed lines unwritten. Still went to work on the music. Sometime in 1938 he was ready to set the missing lines. Repeated letters to Hughes did not elicit the needed language, forcing Still to suspend work and turn to other projects (including *Song of a City* for the New York World's Fair, the ballet *Miss Sally's Party*, and *A Bayou Legend*, his third opera). All in all, he delayed putting the finishing touches on the opera for several years, finally turning to the less experienced Arvey to supply the missing lines. The work was completed only in 1941.

At that point there were not many options for getting an opera produced, for there were only three permanent companies in the United States. Still began by sending the score to the Metropolitan Opera, which returned it with a form rejection letter. World War II slowed his campaign, but in spring of 1944 Still showed the score to conductor Leopold Stokowski, who had previously introduced several of his symphonic works. Stokowski had achieved fame for his leadership of the Philadelphia Orchestra; he had become a popular icon even before his involvement with Walt Disney's 1941 *Fantasia*, an enormously popular feature-length animated cartoon that was underscored with classical music. Stokowski was impressed with the opera and undertook to champion it.

A New Opera Company

The New York City Center of Music and Drama and its brand-new constituent members, the New York City Symphony and its companion New York City Opera, were unexpected, belated legacies from the Great Depression of the 1930s. Unpaid taxes had left the city as reluctant owner of a cavernous, formerly Masonic theater in midtown Manhattan. Taking imaginative advantage of what was something of a white elephant, the city leased the building to a new nonprofit group—the City Center—with the mandate that the former Shriners' theater would provide a home for low-cost, high-quality entertainment "for the people." Such a center was a longtime goal of Progressive-era activists; it had been modeled in the 1930s by the Federal Music Project and made more urgent in wartime. "For the people" was more than a slogan; of the ten original guarantors who each "loaned" at least $5,000 to get the City Center of Music and Drama started, four were unions, indicating unusually broad-based (if still largely white) local support for the ambitious project.[6]

Laszlo Halasz conducted the company's first opera, Puccini's *Tosca*, early in 1944, thus inaugurating its two-a-year, spring and fall seasons that were spaced just before and after the Met's long-established winter season. The higher-profile Stokowski, who volunteered to become the first conductor of the new orchestra, directed a series of concerts in early 1944. He wrote to Still in May, proposing to conduct first a suite from the opera with the new orchestra, which he believed would lead to a full-length concert performance, and then to a fully staged production, which he hoped would be taken to other cities. In the fall he gave a press conference to present his plans for the new season. Trading on the longed-for prospect of an end to the war in Europe, he announced that he would conduct "a new series of operas" in the spring. "Already selected are one by Darius Milhaud called *Bolivar*, which deals with the South American hero, and another by William Grant Still called *Troubled Island*, with an all-Negro cast, the action taking place on Haiti in the eighteenth century, in the days of Toussaint L'Ouverture."[7] (It is worth pointing out here that Stokowski was never the director of the City Center's opera company. He was never in a formal position to set the opera company's repertoire. His initial plans were therefore, presumably, for less-expensive unstaged concert performances, to be given by the orchestra.)

Nine months later, the war in Europe ended. Somehow, the plans for *Troubled Island* became more grandiose. A national campaign was announced to raise $30,000, with Eleanor Roosevelt as its honorary chair. Not only would the opera be produced (and staged) in New York, this sum would guarantee the costs of a tour to "the principal cities of the country." The Stills' hopes for the opera, and even for some resulting prosperity, soared; they even looked at new houses in suburban Ojai.

A year later, in July 1946, the picture had changed. Little money had been raised, not even enough for the local production. Moreover, Stokowski had left the City Center and its orchestra. (Financial issues and turf rivalry with Halasz, the difficult director of the opera company, which shared personnel with the orchestra, are likely causes.) Now the donors were told that the opera would be produced in the regular opera season (with Halasz conducting) during 1946–47, if just $20,000 could be raised. A tour was still possible—provided the necessary financial backing materialized. The reality was that the fund-raising campaign had fizzled. Stokowski, Still's erstwhile champion, was now bereft of any conducting platform at the City Center, whether orchestral or operatic; of necessity he had abandoned the campaign.

Far away from the action, Still watched all this from the West Coast and fumed as the 1946–47 seasons went by with no *Troubled Island*. In March, he wrote to City Center board chairman Newbold Morris, asking why *Troubled Island* was projected to cost $15,000 when other operas the company had produced had cost four to six thousand. He dramatically dissociated himself from Stokowski's projection of an "all-Negro" cast, even suggesting a connection between this notion and the high projected cost: ". . . unless someone, in an effort to spread false propaganda about *Troubled Island* and thus to insure its non-production, has spread the rumor that it must be done with an all-Negro cast." Still claimed in this letter to have turned down productions with all-Negro casts, and stated that he needed only three African Americans to be part of the production; he named Larry Whisonant, baritone; Camilla Williams, soprano; and Syvilla Fort as choreographer. (The rest could be filled by whites using blackface, a longstanding, common theatrical practice just coming into disrepute.) From his location in anti-union Los Angeles, Still added a gratuitous and thoroughly unwelcome political opinion: "I am not concerned, as are many so-called 'liberals,' with creating jobs for the greatest possible number of people, whether they qualify or not . . . [there are now] but a small number of colored people who are capable of singing in the operatic style in which *Troubled Island* is written . . ."[8] Still expressed his determination that *Troubled Island* should be treated as an opera rather than as a musical. This had implications for the voices and the venue, but his reasons transcended those issues. There had been plenty of all-black Broadway productions, dating back a half-century; Still had been involved in several of them earlier in his career. It was not his goal to bring Broadway to the opera house; it was his goal to succeed in European-style opera, a genre that had held the stage in America for generations, and one in which no American before him, black or white, had unequivocally succeeded. (There were still arguments about whether Gershwin's *Porgy and Bess*, with its black subject and its use of jazz rhythms, was really an opera, an indication of the height of the barriers Still sought to surmount.)

Still's string of successful symphonic performances now extended over almost two decades. He was at the height of his powers. This was his moment of opportunity, already delayed for eight years. The unnecessarily provocative text of this letter may be taken as an expression of his frustration as the promise of a production seemed to fade from the realm of the possible. (It *was* seen as provocative and offensive; Newbold Morris, president of the City Center and the addressee, forwarded it to Morton Baum, the company's treasurer, who made it one of his rare inclusions in his lengthy typescript memoir of the City Center's early years.)

Remarkably, the company soon decided to accept Stokowski's artistic judgment (if not his leadership) and produce *Troubled Island* as part of its regular season, without the extra funds (by then long returned to their donors). This was a courageous decision on the part of the opera company, which was in a tough struggle for survival. In the six months before the production of *Troubled Island*, several elements of the City Center's year-round calendar, essential to its continued existence, were withdrawn or severely shaken. After its five-year startup period, the organization was negotiating an organizational and financial transition that made the decision to produce *Troubled Island* a particularly risky one.[9] That explains the low-budget production values. It also made Still's hostile 1947 letter and his split with Hughes all the harder for management, which had depended on widespread cooperation and good will, for it encouraged others, including paying audiences and critics, to take sides.

New frustrations arose even after the decision was made. This time they came from Still himself, for he now insisted that Arvey receive fifteen percent of the librettist's royalty. Hughes, who by this time was pretty frustrated himself, resisted at first, and the necessary contracts remained unsigned. The conflict may have kept the opera out of the fall 1948 season. The issue was settled only in February, less than two months before the actual premiere, after Heinz Condell, the company's set designer, had already started work on the sets. A few days before the production, Still chose to go public with his dispute over the libretto, publishing an account of his collaboration in the *Times* that took Hughes to task for not finishing the job and implied that he would rather work with his wife: "The inevitable need for additions, changes and deletions occurred as work progressed, but Langston Hughes was not near to assist . . . I then turned to my wife, who writes professionally under the name of Verna Arvey, to pinch-hit for Mr. Hughes. She did it so well that my libretto problem was solved."[10] It is more than likely that Arvey drafted both the 1947 letter and the preperformance *Times* story. Regrettably, both may have discouraged some of his potential audience and diverted attention away from the achievement that the production of *Troubled Island* represented.

||||

Three performances were scheduled, the usual number for any production. In spite of all the changes, the Stills continued to expect that *Troubled Island* would be given added performances, maybe even allowed to run for a while after the opera season ended, as Menotti's double bill had done a few months earlier, after the fall 1948 season. The opening night audience was ecstatic, further raising their hopes. Later audiences, however, were reportedly less so. The third and final performance, conducted by the young Julius Rudel, with many substitutions in the cast, closed the company's season and did not draw a large audience. There was no apparent demand for further performances, and none were scheduled; in

Musical rehearsal of Troubled Island. *Laszlo Halasz (seated, next to the piano) is conducting; Still is to his right. The pianist is Julius Rudel, later Musical Director of the New York City Opera. This sketch by George Mann Schellhase appeared in the* New York Times, *March 27, 1949, along with a story by critic Olin Downes, as part of the runup to the premiere. Used by permission of the estate of George Mann Shellhase.*

any case, the theater was already booked. Optimistic talk of further productions by other companies continued for a while but came to nothing.

Both Still and Arvey (who did not go to New York for the premiere) were thrilled in the short term and devastated by the letdown that followed. Their long-term response was to develop what I have called the "plot theory," that a communist-inspired, race-based plot aimed explicitly at Still led to the opera's poor reviews and thus dashed any hopes for more performances or for the major breakthrough in American race relations that they wanted those performances to bring. They claimed that the critics had met and plotted to pan the opera, and that one of their number came to Still's hotel room the night before the premiere to warn him of the collective decision. Yet the critic they long named as the messenger, Howard Taubman of the *New York Times*, wrote that he had not been able to meet Still at all.[11] The noxious combination of race prejudice, reflected here in critical confusion generated by longstanding theatrical stereotypes, along with the continuing, more general prejudice against new "American" operas, was more than enough to sink *Troubled Island*. Still's public break with Hughes and the political tenor of the time helped to seal its fate.

The City Center's administrators were divided in their response. Morton Baum, the financial officer, perhaps wearied by the years of conflict that preceded the production, commented in his unpublished memoir, "'Troubled Island' received a cool reception. It was clear that the music did not measure up in strength to the libretto. Such is the inherent risk of any new work—untried on the stage. At any rate, an American composer had been given an opportunity to be heard."[12] In a much later telephone interview, Julius Rudel, the rehearsal conductor for the production, who became the long-time director of the company and would, along with Morton Baum, have had a say in whether the opera would be revived, seems to have had doubts about whether it would "arouse the house."[13] On the other hand, Jean Dalrymple, the City Center's publicist, also a key figure in the early operation of the City Center, wrote effusively (though somewhat later) that it was "splendidly produced and extraordinarily well-cast."[14] Unfortunately for Still, Dalrymple was outvoted by Baum and Rudel.

Published critical response to the opera was mixed. The critics asked, was it really an opera, or was it "merely" an operetta? (White critics had had the same problem with Gershwin's *Porgy and Bess* more than a decade earlier.) A few critics raised questions about whether the characterizations of individuals portrayed in the opera were sufficiently well drawn. Olin Downes, the influential *Times* music critic, had both good things and bad to say about the opera. They reveal both his race-bound expectations and a related uncertainty about what American opera ought to look and sound like. He balanced his opening putdown of "a good many clichés of Broadway and Hollywood" with "as the piece goes on, there is evident in it an operatic talent, a structure of considerable breadth and melodic curve which commends the opera to the audience . . ." He liked the final scene, where "Mr. Still comes nearer to exotic folksong and popular rhythms than he does anywhere else in the score," yet he saw Azelia's closing aria as anticlimactic. Summing up, he wrote, "there is enough that is broadly melodious, enough that supplies dramatic movement on the stage, enough of operatic architecture to make the opera as a whole entertaining and to justify, in all probability, a good number of repetitions before the season closes."[15] Sadly, he was wrong in this prediction.

One private response is suggestive. Hughes did not join Still and the cast to acknowledge the applause at the end of the opera. His biographer reports that he hovered at intermission in hopes of judging audience response, was rewarded with a comment about the cheapness of the costumes, and made himself scarce at the end. Carl Van Vechten, the most prominent white patron and facilitator of the Harlem Renaissance, wrote to him a few days later:

> Where WERE YOU? . . . The music is conventional (and so, to be frank, is the book) and rather light opera-ish, but it is tuneful and never dull. The direction was appallingly bad. With better direction the music and book would both be brightened considerably. The orchestral direction was brilliant. . . . Marie Powers [Azelia], a great actress and singer in other roles was completely miscast and frankly pretty Godawful. More like a windmill than a Negro.
>
> The natural ending of the opera and a terrifically ironic and stunning one would have been the robbing of the body by the street-boys. What follows is completely anti-climactic . . .

Van Vechten's letter ends with a comment on the casting that balances those already quoted from Still and Dalrymple: "The whole thing would be better done by Negroes, but it is very important to impress upon repertory musical theatres the idea that it is not necessary to engage a Negro company to give a Negro opera." His conclusion turns out to have been wishful thinking, however: "I think more will be heard of this work."[16]

Was the opera really "closed down," as Still's family continues to claim? The answer is an unequivocal no. New operas were regularly scheduled for three performances by this company. A few were revived in later seasons or, backed by a clear demand for tickets, given extra performances if scheduling of both theater and cast permitted. In one case (an earlier revival of Massenet's *Werther*), the third performance was canceled; that definitely did not happen with *Troubled Island*. The letter of the opera company's commitment was exactly fulfilled, though Stokowski's earlier extravagant promises were not and could not be. What is more likely is that the management of "the people's house" took its decision to produce

Troubled Island in order to assert the company's allegiance to its first principles in the face of multiple pressures, including but not limited to the financial and the political.

To this latter-day listener, *Troubled Island* has some magnificent musical high points, among them "To the Hills," the chorus that closes the first act; Martel's "I Dream a World" and the love duet between the plotters in the second; and, despite its unhappy positioning, Azelia's lament at the end of the opera. From a dramatic point of view, the singer playing Azelia found it impossibly difficult to hold the audience through the lament, for it comes after the action has ended, that is, after the murder of Dessalines and the departure of the plotters. In addition, the efforts at comic relief probably set up expectations that threw the audience (and maybe the performers as well) off balance. This would apply to the chorus "To polish and shine" that opens the second act, and most particularly to the byplay between the (male) fishermen and the (female) fruit vendors that opens the final scene. In the revisions he made in the score following the production, Still eliminated this byplay; he also made Azelia's task somewhat easier by allowing Dessalines to survive long enough to exchange a few words with her before her lament.

|||

There is a postscript, one that isn't mentioned in the Still papers or Arvey's *In One Lifetime*, though both partners must have been aware of it. In 1957, the Ford Foundation announced a grant of $105,000 to the New York City Opera, which had produced a few more new operas after *Troubled Island* but was always hampered by its financial limitations. The grant underwrote two spring seasons entirely made up of operas composed by Americans "in the last thirty years." The company did not attempt a better-financed, more polished revival of *Troubled Island*, even though it had already helped develop a number of black singers who might have taken more of its roles effectively. Nor did it produce a second opera by Still, as it did for several other composers who had no more success than he with their first operas. (Robert Ward and Lee Hoiby come to mind.) Again, in 1962, there was correspondence with the Ford Foundation about a possible tour of the USSR and Eastern Europe by the company. (The Stills could not have known this.) Morton Baum's letter listing operas the company had already produced did not include *Troubled Island*, or, for that matter, several others. More tellingly, Baum added a group of four additional operas that might be presented if the Foundation would put up a larger sum to underwrite the tour; these four might feature "Negro" casts. All four were composed by white male composers on black subjects:

Show Boat (Jerome Kern); *Lost in the Stars* (Kurt Weill); *The Emperor Jones* (Louis Gruenberg); and *Porgy and Bess* (George Gershwin). The tour did not take place, but it is clear from this letter that *Troubled Island* had dropped out of the operatic loop, and that there was no place for Still's voice in opera. Black singers, yes; a story about blacks, yes; black composer William Grant Still, no. If part of that resulted from the Stills' intransigence about possible revisions or their political position, the punishment was both excessive and destructive.

The 1949 production was initially a triumph and a major landmark, but a great deal about this so-called "breakthrough" production showed just how much breaking through had not yet taken place. The barrier, breached once, quickly closed over; the operatic audience and the country turned—as did the Stills—to other issues, some of them presaged by the circumstances surrounding *Troubled Island*. We continue to await the more sympathetic production that will allow it to speak to historical issues of race beyond their localized 1940s context.

9 | Moscow's "Subtle but Effective Hand"

AFTER THE 1949 PRODUCTION of *Troubled Island*, performances of the symphonic music on which Still had come to rely for his income dropped off. The decline was the more significant because Still had largely abandoned his arranging business, and the film industry had largely abandoned him. What happened to bring about this reversal of fortune is a matter for discussion, but there were several elements. Part of it was a matter of changing public taste, for by now a new, post–World War II generation of musicians, conductors and composers had emerged, bringing with them new concepts ranging from bebop and R & B to serialism and the music of chance. (The postwar audience, too, had changed.) Part of it was the result of larger political and social issues, and part of it had to do with Still's own choices. Here I will consider the political issues—mainly involving anticommunism and race in their peculiar symbiosis—along with the personal and associated artistic choices, going back to the start of the *Troubled Island* project.[1]

The wide-ranging political and social debates that had addressed both racial and economic injustice in the Depression years became sharply polarized following the end of World War II. A wave of anticommunism engulfed the body politic in the late 1940s as the Cold War began in earnest. Under the attention-getting leadership of Senator Joseph McCarthy, anticommunists mounted a broad attack on almost anyone who had ever flirted, however briefly, with communism, involving many of those who had made up the centrist New Deal coalition that had formed around Franklin D. Roosevelt. Liberals, progressives, socialists, and others who had never been involved with the Communist Party (and who had often opposed it) had to cope with often exaggerated anticommunist claims that advocacy of racial and economic justice within the United States meant support of the Soviet cause against American interests. The ensuing wave swirled around the arts community, definitely including the New York City Opera and its parent City Center. "Left of center . . . was almost taken for granted" among the composers whose works were produced there, as Julius Rudel told this interviewer later on.[2] The sensational coverage of communist-versus-anticommunist activities had immediate consequences for Still's opera. In the week before the premiere of *Troubled Island*, for example, New York's front pages were given over to a Cultural and Scientific Congress for World Peace whose main feature was an appearance by the prominent Soviet composer Dmitri Shostakovich. (Shostakovich's music was popular with American symphony audiences.) Indicative of the public hysteria, the FBI "detained" three Canadian conference attendees on the grounds of alleged communist activity and expelled two of them on the spot.

| | |

Still had long done his best to ignore politics, along with most other things that didn't impinge directly on his musical commitments and aspirations. He had pursued his own goals with a determined single-mindedness that had persisted through thick and thin, the only way he could have achieved what he did. As Carlton Moss remembered it, "He never talked about anything else but that music . . . he was always off, in another world."[3] That doesn't mean that he was entirely unaware of his surroundings. Of course he had known about Marcus Garvey, the NAACP, and the political issues of the 1920s and 1930s, for he must have stumbled across them as he rode the subway and walked the streets of Manhattan. (He was aware enough to vote, for example.) He had to have taken at least some note of his surroundings in order to negotiate them successfully; he just didn't choose to give them more than minimal attention.

In fact, his commitment to the race and to humankind in general was absolute, as was his belief that he could express that commitment through his music. As long ago as in the "Personal Notes," he had written of the *Afro-American Symphony*, "My Opinion: This symphony approaches but does not attain to the profound symphonic work such as I hope to write; a work presenting a great truth that will be of value to mankind in general."[4] He believed that *Troubled Island*, too, would make a real difference in race relations. This idealism led him, in the 1940s, after he had remarried and was living in Los Angeles, to break with his own practice of speaking only about, or through, his music. He did it by becoming involved in the anticommunist movement. Why he chose that route, and why just then, is not entirely clear. Langston Hughes, who was more political and who did flirt briefly with communism, may have taken him to a leftist meeting or two in Los Angeles while they worked together on *Troubled Island*. Verna Arvey, who kept her maiden name after their marriage, filled numerous scrapbooks with anticommunist columns and articles; she very likely had much to do with his new activism.

In Los Angeles, liberated—and consequently isolated—from the noise and crush and pressure of New York, Still came to associate communism with the modernists' dissonant techniques that he had abandoned some years earlier out of his race-influenced need to communicate effectively with his audience. (A little later, in the Depression years, many of the white modernists followed suit, not for racially inspired reasons but in the hope of reaching a wider audience across class lines. In the 1920s, some politicians had already associated the "ultramodern" with decadent European anarchism and socialism. Still seems to have accepted that connection later on.) Presently he became convinced that there was a direct connection between the advocates of modernist styles and the threat of foreign domination posed by the Communist Party. As the country emerged from World War II, he bought into the notion of shadowy, communist-inspired conspiracies that controlled the movie and recording industries, keeping his music from being heard and preventing him from getting the concert commissions and commercial work that, on the basis of his earlier experience, should have provided his livelihood. Since some critics had made negative comments about his "universal" style, he came to the position that those who had criticized his work or passed him over for various opportunities were involved in a grand communist conspiracy to destroy American music. His growing suspicions were another reason for his split with Hughes.

A much more direct explanation for the problems Still met, one that he found very difficult to face, was the institutionally grounded racism that pervaded American society and permeated individual attitudes. Early on, his crusade to achieve recognition as a composer of concert music and opera had seemed quixotic in the face of that racism, but he was extremely gifted, and his work was welcomed in the struggling modernist community. Later, his achievements brought him into direct competition with the developing modernist concert musical establishment, which was for the most part politically liberal or progressive. (In general, white music makers, including critics and audiences, were struggling with anti-Semitism at the time; black-white racism was not even on the radar in terms of moving toward real shared power.)

Still went public with his plot theory only after *Troubled Island* was passed over by the City Center in 1946, though there were earlier hints. He had begun with an obscure, relatively innocuous article entitled "Politics in Music," in which he railed at the "cerebral pseudo-music" of various modernists and at those "who subordinate their art to political propaganda."[5] Privately he associated the leading modernists, who had become critical of his music starting in 1936, with communist subversion. An October 1949 diary entry read "Disquieting news re the persecution we are receiving from the Communists. Unfortunately we cannot tell people of this because they would not believe us." Three months later he reluctantly added, "I hate to be forced to admit that racial prejudice entered into it." He wrote to Richard Nixon, then a young congressman, detailing what he believed to be communist activity in the world of music. He asked to testify at the notorious Hollywood hearings held by the House Committee on Un-American Activities in 1951. (He was turned down, then and later, partly because he never had anything concrete to report.) By then the "cerebral pseudo-music" had become in his mind a communist plot to destroy American music. In 1953, he made the last of several public speeches on the topic to the San Jose, California, Chamber of Commerce. "It is true," he claimed, "that Moscow has had a subtle but effective hand in our arts for many years." Then he named some of those through whom he believed Moscow's hand was operating, including (among others) several prominent modernist composers with whom he had aesthetic differences, conductors who had not performed his music, certain African American musicians, critics who had attacked his music, unnamed functionaries of phonograph companies that had failed to record his work, and others connected in one way or another with the City Center for Music and Drama.[6] What led him to these uncharacteristic outbursts? I would argue that they had more to do with the frustrations he was encountering in his career than with a sudden interest in political theory.

III

Still's anticommunist position, so antithetical to that of most people involved with the arts (most of them definitely not communists, though many were more interested in politics than he) probably influenced the later reception of his music and discouraged cultural critics from evaluating his creative position. Thus it becomes increasingly important to separate his views from those of his second wife, Verna Arvey, who helped him give voice to his political position. It also becomes much more difficult to separate his views from hers, for they were often expressed through writing that appears to have originated with her. A 1940 exchange of letters with Charles Seeger, writing as an editor for the Conference of Inter-American Relations in the Field of Music, clarifies that Still was entirely willing for Arvey to speak on his behalf, even over his name. She had submitted an article she had written in response to a request to him from Seeger, who replied to Still, "I had hoped to have something directly from your hand." Seeger added that he would require some changes if he was to publish Arvey's essay. Still's reply defended Arvey's submission and established her unequivocally as his spokesperson: "Miss Arvey has worked with me for quite a while and has always been accurate in expressing exactly what I want to say. For me, this is the best possible arrangement. So you see that her article is really mine. I gave her the material and approved of the finished product. If you wish to change it, please do so *only to the extent* of deleting proper names. You see, if it is altered too much, it will cease to be mine . . ."[7] Editorial changes such as Seeger requested are, for most people, a normal part of the publishing process; this statement suggests, at best, an unusual naïveté.

In the early years of their association, Arvey's language is readily distinguished from Still's. His writing tends to be concise, formally correct, and (generally) tactful, while hers is more often less gracious and given to risky generalizations that are not required by the subject. A key example of this comes from the run-up to the *Troubled Island* production, where the "false propaganda" and "so-called 'liberals'" remarks in the 1947 letter quoted in the previous chapter seem out of character for Still himself. Still's decision to allow Arvey to speak for him in every particular creates problems for his biographers. One writer, Jon Michael Spencer, addresses the conundrum of language created by Arvey but attributed to Still by referring to "two indivisible people who became William Grant Still."[8] In reaching that formulation, Spencer begs the larger question of the dynamics of the couple's relationship, its racial inflections, and its implications for Still's career. On the other hand, he avoids the pitfall of blaming Arvey for actions that were, ultimately, Still's responsibility, even when they were expressed in her words rather than his own.

The anticommunist outbursts could be dismissed as sour grapes, but their racial implications were important. The aesthetic dilemma created by his racial position was profound and inescapable. Virtually all African American artists of Still's time faced the problem of how to maintain their personal integrity in the face of the necessity of performing for white audiences in the face of the stereotyped roles and genres assigned them by those audiences. (Black jazz bands, yes; racially mixed jazz bands, rarely; black symphony musicians, no; black opera singers, just beginning to appear in numbers in the 1940s.) For his part, Still had composed and arranged for white audiences and conductors almost continuously after his first successes with Sissle and Blake, W. C. Handy, Florence Mills, and Black Swan. He was intimately familiar with the inflections of race and class and the multiple cultural stereotypes, not so much from reading and thinking about them (although no doubt he had done some of that), but from the continuing experiences of his everyday personal and professional life. He was fully aware of his own anomalous position as an African American composer of concert music and of the series of "firsts" and racial breakthroughs he had achieved, or else he could not have arrived at the remarkably original and subtle mix of cultural elements that had gone into his music.

For her part, Arvey certainly struggled with these issues, but her own experience of otherness in American society was, quite simply, different. If there is any conclusion to be drawn, it would be that Arvey had taken on, with Still's blessing, an extraordinarily difficult task in assuming the burden of his correspondence, one that would have left her open to criticism no matter what she did. Part of the hostility that shows up was defensive, for she had the greatest difficulty in meeting the biggest challenge faced by African Americans in the America of Still's time, not to allow "conditions" to defeat them in spirit. Arvey had been deeply hurt by the opposition to her marriage from the African American community. Nothing in her earlier life could have prepared her for the role she was to play, especially those aspects in which black-white race relations played a part. The solution, coming partly from her own inclination and partly from their mutual admiration and their genuine wish to protect each other, was to live, and therefore to reach their political conclusions, in relative isolation.

In leaving New York City and marrying Arvey, Still had to some degree lost touch with both the New Negro movement and the creative ferment of the white modernists, even while his own creativity continued to flourish. More to the point, Still and Arvey, in the case of the *Troubled Island* production, were out of touch with the political and cultural realities of New York City and of the New York City Center of Music and Drama. Had he not been drawn into it through Stokowski's championing of the opera, Still might have avoided the New York City Opera altogether, leaving the opera unproduced. The cultural battles of the left and right in American politics were incorporated willy-nilly in the arguments about *Troubled Island*, including some specific issues that emerged following its production. For example, why was the recording of the dress rehearsal, made for the Voice of America, withdrawn after only one broadcast over one station in Europe? Arvey made this into a race-based, communist plot against Still's "true-blue American" position. But it may just as well have been an act of resistance to Langston Hughes's well-known leftist views, coming from an agency known for its vigorous anticommunism. The opera's plot—about a revolution in which blacks killed their white erstwhile owners—may have become too radical for the moment when the opera actually reached the stage. The mostly white audience may have found it difficult to relate to a plot in which educated mixed-race characters used their skills to systematically undermine the revolution of the proletariat. It is clear that political issues helped shape the politically charged atmosphere in which Still's opera was heard. His outspoken political position may have played a role, right along with his musical decisions about style in the declining interest in his music after 1949. After all, opera, especially opera produced on a grand scale, has always been surrounded by aesthetic, intellectual, and political arguments in addition to the broader social and cultural context in which all the arts are experienced. Still's opera was no exception; moreover, the same issues almost certainly influenced the numerous decisions that left his later operas unproduced for decades, despite the excellence of their music.

Of course race played a major role in the growth and then the unraveling of Still's career, as it did for other black composers. Still wanted to be thought of as a composer who happened to be African American. That was a luxury he seldom enjoyed. More often, he was seen as a black person who happened to be a composer, and who insisted on composing concert music. His sophisticated representations of himself and of his cultural position did not fit the stereotypes. They were, in fact, unique to the man. It is unimaginable that his work could have come from the pen of a white composer in the same time and place. Unfortunately, neither Still nor Arvey provided the verbal expositions or aesthetic pronouncements that might have led to an understanding of his position, then or now. Forsythe had written of "your peculiar isolation from your race" many years earlier; his inability to follow through with an explanation was a great loss for us. It was somehow easier to accept the notion of a specific, politically inspired plot aimed directly at Still than to admit the reality of the monumental racial barriers of the time. For a long time, after all, he had thrown himself at those barriers with remarkable individual success.

In the course of this adventure with public anticommunism and the pressures that led to it, Still came as close to breaking as he ever would.

10 | After the Storm

MUCH HAD HAPPENED in Still's life between the composition of *Troubled Island* (1937–41) and its production: divorce, remarriage, two more children, two more operas and three more symphonies completed, and the list goes on. The children from his second marriage, Duncan Allen (b. 1940), and Judith Anne (b. 1942) were a source of particular delight, reinforcing the contrast between the circumstances of his life in Los Angeles and the old days with Grace.

Still had weathered the Great Depression of the 1930s surprisingly well. Arvey had agreed that he should devote himself entirely to composition, depending mainly on his fellowships and royalties from performances of his symphonic music for their income. Therefore, he took on steadily fewer arranging assignments and—perhaps remembering the long hours the Wilberforce faculty had worked—declined to take on regular students or seek a regular teaching position. He adopted a routine of composing in the mornings and orchestrating his work in the afternoons. He was one of the first to acquire—and use, despite its awkwardness—a music typewriter in the mid-1930s, just one sign of his consistent interest in new technology. It was a mark of success that he could be a full-time composer, even one on a tight budget, for few of his contemporaries, especially those with families, had that luxury.

For her part, Arvey kept the children out of his hair while he composed, used her keyboard skills to play over his newly composed work, made herself available to provide lyrics for the opera plots they devised together, and served as hostess when it was time to entertain friends and relations. In addition, she took care of his voluminous correspondence; wrote publicity, biographical articles, and even books; and (sometimes overzealously) protected his composing time by keeping callers at bay. She made the best of what income they had; in fact, she was as careful with their money as Grace had been casual. Still himself tended the garden he planted in their backyard and made model sets for his operas (most of these apparently lost), and he crafted model trains and two-sided picture puzzles for his children when store-bought toys did not fit into the budget. Despite Still's deep religious convictions, they did not affiliate with a church. Presently they formed a circle of friends with whom they had regular séances, for Still's interest in numerology and the occult did not wane.[1] All in all, they lived together in an idealized, if sometimes threadbare, cocoon, one that was penetrated by relatively few people. Eventually their isolation, like their anticommunism, became problematic.

Royalties, even though there were numerous performances of his compositions, provided an uncertain income, especially with the new mouths to feed. The financial squeeze became steadily tighter as ASCAP's disbursements shrank and the old economy of accompanying dancers and writing for music magazines that had brought Verna some income all but disappeared in the postwar decades. (At one point in the 1960s, Duncan, by then a graduate student at UC Berkeley with a modest income of his own, even offered to loan money to his parents.) The occasional arranging opportunity that came through other film and TV composers, who well knew Still's abilities, helped tide them over; gifts from relatives and scholarships launched the children's college careers as the time came. Recognition came in the form of a series of honorary degrees from a number of colleges, but these rarely carried stipends, sometimes not even travel money.

Carrying On

Somehow, all of Still's worries about getting performances and supporting his family did not interfere with composing. Controversies could swirl around him, but the music poured forth, seemingly unimpeded. To begin with, there were more operas. After Verna had finished off the *Troubled Island* libretto, he turned to her for more librettos, and she obliged. The topics they chose have a series of multicultural settings, although their plots take progressively less advantage of the cultural differences suggested by these varied settings.

First came *A Bayou Legend*, set in "a primitive community, near a bayou."
A Southern Interlude, a short opera about a married couple of unknown ethnicity and a ne'er-do-well brother, later renamed *Highway 1, U.S.A*, followed the next year. Just before he went east for the final rehearsals and the premiere of *Troubled Island*, Still's searches in the Los Angeles Public Library for a story with a southwestern theme rewarded him with a story about a lost city of gold. This took shape as the excellent *Costaso* even while he was giving his anticommunist speeches and dealing with his deep disappointment. In 1951 came *Mota*, set in central Africa. *The Pillar*, set in a Native American pueblo, followed four years later, followed finally by *Minette Fontaine*, with another Louisiana setting. Like the early *Blue Steel*, none of these has been produced by a major company, although several have had amateur or semiprofessional productions. Each of these operas is put together convincingly and contains individual musical jewels despite the vagaries of their librettos.

In one of her news releases for *Troubled Island*, Arvey wrote, "Comparatively rare in the history of operatic music has been the association of fine composer and fine librettist. In general, one has been weaker than the other, and that fact has prevented the survival of many otherwise worthy works. In William Grant Still and Langston Hughes we have a promising combination."[2] Sadly, Arvey could have been writing about her own contribution, for it must be said that her librettos do not measure up in quality to Still's music. As his expressive range and technical skill grew, hers did not keep pace. Two examples document the increasing disparity.

In *A Bayou Legend*, Bazile, the hero, is in love with the spirit Aurore. (Their duet is a musical high point.) The human Clothilde spurns her suitor Leonce and attempts to ensnare Bazile. When Bazile rejects her, she denounces him to the villagers as a follower of witchcraft and spirits. Bazile is hanged, but his spirit miraculously leaves his body and joins Aurore. Leonce now rejects Clothilde, pronouncing vindictively that not only does he reject her, but "no man" will have her now. *A Bayou Legend* was produced by Opera South in Jackson, Mississippi, in 1974, and broadcast on PBS in 1981 to excellent reviews.

One K. W. Bartlett of the Hamburg State Opera, given the score of *Costaso* to review for possible production, provided a lengthy commentary that highlights the libretto's shortcomings. (In the postwar years, the Hamburg Opera, generously supported by the West German government, produced a number of new operas, some of them radically experimental, attracting major international attention in the process.) In *Costaso*, the commandant of a remote desert town sends his lieutenant (Costaso) on an ill-equipped expedition to find a rumored "golden city," for no reason except to clear the way for him to make a pass at Costaso's wife. Costaso obeys and after some vicissitudes manages to return safely. His virtuous wife's anonymous letter (apparently unsupported by any further evidence) to a distant commander brings about a comeuppance to the lecherous commandant.

Bartlett made it clear that he greatly admired certain musical aspects of the opera: "the really flawless interlocking of drama and lyricism is admirable, there is a wonderful flow of melodic invention, the vocal lines are singable and declamation is on the whole faultless." He added that the music "abounds with powerful expression and . . . casts a spell of a very strange and still impressive kind." He felt that the style of its music might be too "folklorist" and "simple" for the radical tastes of the Hamburg audience, though it might be right for another company. On the other hand, he found the libretto unconvincing on many grounds. He started with the hero, Costaso, who "fails to excite our compassion. . . . He never enters into a conflict in the terms of real drama, he embarks on a mission which is without meaning to us . . . Furthermore, the mental attitude Costaso shows in complying with his orders is one of blind obedience—and for this we have no more patience after two world wars and we look upon such attitude rather with contempt than with sympathy . . ."[3] Despite his reservations, Bartlett thought the libretto could be fixed. Whether Still might have been willing to undertake changes that addressed these issues in the libretto had Arvey consented, we cannot know. We know only that he chose not to, perhaps out of loyalty to her. We also know that *Costaso* contains several compelling numbers, including a stunning tenor-baritone duet that, in the course of a generally indifferent 1992 production seen by this author in Altadena, California, totally won over an initially dubious audience.

Although the operas were not being produced, Still continued to compose them, along with orchestral and chamber music.

|||

Still may have lost much of his national audience, but he still had a strong regional one, as well as the individual musicians for whom he composed. In addition, university orchestras and bands continued to play his music. His piano music (*Three Visions, Seven Traceries*) had been written for Verna; in addition, his friend Louis Kaufman performed (and recorded) the *Suite for Violin and Piano* and *Pastorela*. Like all of his chamber music, the *Miniatures* for flute, oboe, and piano are effectively written for the technical capacities of each instrument, economical in their means, and satisfyingly expressive for the audience.

In this late period, Still cultivated his interest in music education. The Standard School Broadcasts in California performed his music on several occasions.

Hollywood composers, 1948. From left: George Antheil, Eugene Zador, Arthur Bergh, Italo Montemezzi, Miklos Rozsa, Richard Hageman, Still, Igor Stravinsky, Ernst Toch, Louis Gruenberg, Erich Wolfgang Korngold. Courtesy of the Los Angeles Music Center Archives / Otto Rothschild Collection.

Still and Arvey together visited numerous schools in the Los Angeles area, talking about his career, playing tapes of his music (Arvey also played when a piano was available), and encouraging students to work hard and follow their dreams, as he had done. A series of honors came his way; they traveled to receive a half-dozen honorary degrees before Still became too infirm to travel. In his last few years, he could no longer compose, but he relished visits from his daughter and her children, and often played the tapes he had collected of the many performances his music had earned over the years. By the time of his death in 1978, he was living in obscurity, having been out of the public eye for almost three decades.

Opportunities for African Americans had not opened up following World War II. This began to change in the turbulent decade of the 1960s, with the civil rights marches, the Black Power movement, and riots in various cities, including Los Angeles. Like many older African Americans, Still was more than ready for

Still, early 1930s. Music Division, the New York Public Library for the Performing Arts, Astor, Lenox and Tilden Foundations. Used by permission.

progress but was horrified at the violence and unprepared to address the generational and class differences that now emerged so explosively. He detested the notion of black separatism, which he saw as a new form of segregation, and was quite out of sympathy with the young people who were not interested in becoming acquainted with the kind of music he had written and who dismissed the achievements of their elders as "accommodationist." Invited to speak at a meeting at Indiana University in the turbulent 1960s, Still was shouted down. Once more he retreated into his cocoon, having done little in the meantime to get over the old friction about anticommunism, and once more he was alienated, this time from a potential new, younger audience.

In Still we see a creative artist who challenged several different canonic establishments in the course of his career. In the 1920s, black writers left him out of their accounts of respectable "Negro" music. These accounts focused on composers who based their concert music on spirituals, that is, black religious songs, or who made settings of spirituals; most were in respectable occupations such as teaching. At that point, Still was earning his living as a commercial musician, an occupation that was considered lower-class and was ignored by black intellectuals. When he was able to get hearings as a "serious" composer, Still chose to base his work on the (highly disreputable) blues as a more authentically black expression than were the spirituals. That distinction—blues versus the spirituals as the basis for a new kind of concert music—went undiscussed at the time but was in fact a landmark in the single-handed creation by Still of his unique, New Negro–influenced variant of musical high modernism.

Later, after his concert music was widely heard and he was able to negotiate the production of *Troubled Island*, Still chose to take a very public anticommunist position, eventually accusing a number of musicians of Communist Party membership. The accusations were largely unfounded; they drew, and still draw, considerable resentment. Finally, late in his career, he publicly resisted the Black Power movement, partly because of his anticommunism, but more fundamentally because of its advocacy of black separatism and its focus on only one aspect of the black musical experience. If the black intelligentsia of the 1920s was unaware of the concert music scene on which Still made a splash and disdained him for his commercial affiliations, its counterparts four decades later were even more oblivious to that history, considering it part of a culture they rejected across the board. Both of these political positions have had the result that he continues to escape the scrutiny of many African American cultural critics.

Still's positions continue to challenge us. Here was a composer who identified, and was identified in American culture, as Afro-American, who became a major figure of the Harlem Renaissance, and who *left* the "black" world of popular music-making in order to compose symphonies, ballets, and operas just as these same genres were becoming so thoroughly entrenched as elite, white-only cultural markers. Here was a musician who *left* the world of jazz at the moment when many of his erstwhile colleagues were turning their ghettoization to advantage, making it into the very hallmark of black success in a notoriously oppressive culture. Yet his music, like his career, is clearly stamped with his cultural position as an African American. Here was a musical pioneer, one who achieved artistic success in the face of longstanding racial barriers and offered a beacon for all the "others" in American culture at the moment it was most needed. And, here was a citizen whose political positions are, to say the least, confrontational. Finally, here was a composer who really did achieve what he sought. He became "another American voice," one who spoke compellingly across the genres and across the years, and one who continues to speak to us.

NOTES

CHAPTER 1: An Uncertain Ovation

1. For two recent accounts of this tradition, see Mellonee V. Burnim and Portia K. Maultsby, eds., *African American Music: An Introduction* (New York: Routledge, 2006), especially chapter 8, "Art/Classical Music: Chronological Overview," by Josephine R. B. Wright, and "Interpreting Classical Music," by Olly Wilson; see also Eileen Southern, *The Music of Black Americans*, 3rd ed. (New York: Norton, 1997). The tradition goes far beyond the operas composed by Harry Lawrence Freeman and Scott Joplin, in 1903 and 1904, respectively.

CHAPTER 2: Still's Arkansas Childhood

1. Xavier Zinzeindolph Wynn, "The Development of African American Schools in Arkansas, 1863–1963: A Historical Comparison of Black and White Schools with Regard to Funding and the Quality of Education" DEd, Univ. of Mississippi, 1995, reports the following (74, 76):

AVERAGES FOR 1909–10	WHITE TEACHERS	BLACK TEACHERS
Monthly salaries in Ark.	$40.52	$30.36
Number of school days	94 days	70 days

AVERAGE FOR 1914–15	WHITE STUDENTS	BLACK STUDENTS
Expenditure per student	$8.15	$3.74

2. Real estate records, Wilkinson County Courthouse, Woodville, MS.

3. William Grant Still, "Personal Notes," undated typescript (c. 1932), published in Catherine Parsons Smith, *William Grant Still: A Study in Contradictions* (Berkeley and Los Angeles: University of California Press, 2000), hereafter *ASC*, 215–16. For another overview of Little Rock in Still's youth, see Willard B. Gatewood, "The Formative Years of William Grant Still: Little Rock, Arkansas, 1895–1911," *ASC*, 21–38.

4. Ownership details are documented in the Arkansas History Commission, State Capitol, Little Rock.

5. Fon Louise Gordon, untitled, *Pulaski County Historical Review*, vol. 35, no. 2 (Summer 1987): 26–29. Gibbs was located at Wolf and West 11th Sts. The first of Carrie's

productions was said to be Shakespeare; later productions were called "extravaganzas." In 1918 and 1919 they rented the Kempner Theater for two nights for the production. The Kempner was the main theater in Little Rock, and black people were thrilled to be able to sit downstairs.

6. "Personal Notes," *ASC*, 217.

7. Ibid., 216.

8. Ibid., 216–17.

9. Ibid., 217.

10. Harold Bruce Forsythe, "A Study in Contradictions," undated typescript, c. 1932, published in *ASC*, 283.

11. "Personal Notes," *ASC*, 216.

12. Washington's "Atlanta Exposition" speech was published in his autobiography, *Up from Slavery* (Garden City, N.Y.: 1900), 218–25, and is also available online at http://docsouth .unc.edu/fpn/washington/washing.html. W. E. Burghardt DuBois, *The Souls of Black Folk*, (Chicago: A. C. McClurg, 1903), is available online at http://www.bartleby.com/114/.

13. Letter, J. H. Fears to Booker T. Washington, Aug. 13, 1914, reports that "a student" at Gibbs reported taking English, 4 semesters; Algebra, 2; Geometry, 2; History, 2: Civics/Government, 1; Physics, 1; Chemistry, 1; Zoology, 1/2; Botany, 1/2; Psychology, 1; Agriculture, 1; Physical Geology, 1. MSS 00–10, Ser IV B4, f36, Black Arkansiana Collection, Butler Center, Little Rock Public Library. Petition from black citizens in Record Book E, School Board Minutes, Sept. 27, 1910, 66, Black Arkansiana Collection. Also reported in *Arkansas Gazette*, Aug. 4, 1910, 10.

14. Shepperson's obituary appeared in the *Arkansas Gazette*, Aug. 18, 1922, 8.

15. Carrie Shepperson's will is filed at the Arkansas History Commission.

CHAPTER 3: An Ohio Apprenticeship

1. Letter, William Grant Still and Verna Arvey Papers, University of Arkansas–Fayetteville.

2. "Personal Notes," *ASC*, 217.

3. Ibid.

4. Ibid.

5. Faculty Minutes, typed, notebooks, Wilberforce University Library. A more detailed version of the material in this chapter appears in the present author's "William Grant Still in Ohio (1911–1919)," *American Music*, vol. 22 (2004): 203–30.

6. "Personal Notes," *ASC*, 217–18.

7. Verna Arvey, *In One Lifetime* (Fayetteville: University of Arkansas Press, 1984), 44–45.

8. "Negro Serious Music," interview with Still by R. Donald Brown, California State University–Fullerton, Oral History Program, Nov. 13, 1967, and Dec. 4, 1967, 29.

9. Still, "A Composer's Viewpoint," in Robert Haas, ed., *William Grant Still and the Fusion of Cultures in American Music* (Los Angeles: Black Sparrow Press, 1975), 128.

10. "Personal Notes," *ASC*, 218.

11. *Oberlin Conservatory Bulletin*, 1916–1918.

12. "Personal Notes," *ASC*, 218.

13. Ibid., 218–19.

14. *The Freeman*, May 13, 1916, 5.

CHAPTER 4: New York City

1. "Personal Notes," *ASC*, 218.

2. Undated letters in Gatti-Casazza correspondence for 1919, Metropolitan Opera Archives. (Dates inferred from postmarks.)

3. For more on Williams and Walker, see Thomas Riis, *Just Before Jazz: Black Musical Theater in New York, 1890–1915* (Washington: Smithsonian Institution Press, 1989.)

4. For more on Florence Mills, see Bill Egan, *Florence Mills, Harlem Jazz Queen* (Lanham, Md.: Scarecrow Press, 2004.)

5. For more on Henderson, se Jeffrey Magee, *The Uncrowned King of Swing: Fletcher Henderseon and Big Band Jazz* (New York: Oxford University Press, 2005).

6. For an account of Black Swan's success and later demise, see Robert M. W. Dixon and John Godrich, *Recording the Blues* (New York: Stein and Day, 1970), 13–16, 26.

7. Useful sources for information on Broadway theatrical productions (though generally not as thorough for black productions) include Gerald M. Bordman, *American Musical Theatre: A Chronicle* (New York: Oxford University Press, 2001); Tommy Krasker, *Catalog of the American Musical* (Washington, D.C.: National Institute for Opera and Musical Theater, 1988); and www.ibdb.com.

8. Letter, Varèse to Dane Rudhyar, Mar. 7, 1928. Rudhyar Collection, Department of Special Collections, Stanford University Library, Stanford University.

9. Carlton Moss, interview with the author and Lance Bowling, Feb. 21, 1993.

10. Olin Downes, *New York Times*, Feb. 9, 1925, quoted in "Personal Notes," *ASC*, 222.

11. Alain Locke, *The New Negro* (New York: Albert & Charles Boni, Inc, 1925; reprint, New York: Macmillan, 1992), 209.

12. "Personal Notes," *ASC*, 226.

13. No awards were given for music in the award's first year, 1926. (That year, the awards were given in late 1926; probably the judges missed the performance of *Darker America*, which was given on Nov. 28. They may have chosen to pass over the performance of *Levee Land* the previous January because of its "popular" component.) The awards for 1927 were presented in early 1928. First prizes went to Clarence Cameron White and Nathaniel Dett, both of whom were senior to Still in terms of recognition. Still's was a second prize. Forsythe's "A Study in Contradictions" was written c. 1932; published in *ASC*, 274–99.

14. Still-Arvey Papers, University of Arkansas–Fayetteville.

CHAPTER 5: Making His Mark

1. Letter in Ruth Page collection, New York Public Library for the Performing Arts, Lincoln Center.

2. For more on Dunham, see Joyce Aschenbrenner, *Katherine Dunham: Dancing a Life* (University of Illinois Press, 2002).

3. See Wayne Shirley, "Religion in Rhythm: William Grant Still's Orchestrations for

Willard Robison's *Deep River Hour,*" *Black Music Research Journal* 19 (1999): 1–42. Scores and parts to many of these are in the Ellington Collection at the Smithsonian Institution and at the Institute for Jazz Studies, Rutgers University, Newark.

4. Letters, Grace Bundy Still to Countee Cullen, Department of Special Collections, Tulane University.

5. Letter, Still to Irving Schwerké, Jan. 9, 1931, text in *ASC*, 238–39.

6. Telephone interview with David William Still, Grace's grandson, Feb. 10, 2005.

CHAPTER 6: Still's Instrumental Music

1. Still, sketchbook, at William Grant Still Music.

2. A more detailed discussion of this symphony, especially the Scherzo movement, is found in *ASC*, 114–51.

3. Aaron Copland, *Our New Music: Leading Composers in Europe and America* (New York and London: Whittlesey House, McGraw-Hill, 1941), 88–89. For more on Copland's cultural situation, see Beth E. Levy, "From Orient to Occident: Aaron Copland and the Sagas of the Prairie," *Aaron Copland and His World*, ed. Carol J. Oja and Judith Tick (Princeton and Oxford: Princeton University Press, 2005), 307–50.

4. Still, "Personal Notes," c. 1932, *ASC*, 128–29.

5. The Jamaica-born Garvey (1887–1940) organized his United Negro Improvement Association in the United States starting in 1918, and was arrested on mail fraud charges in 1922, sent to prison in 1925, and deported to his native Jamaica in 1927. The elements of demagoguery in his practice made him a controversial figure (and a target for the FBI) despite (or possibly because of) his popularity among blacks.

CHAPTER 7: Los Angeles, 1934–

1. Forsythe's essay is published in *ASC*, 274–99. See also Smith, "An Unknown 'New Negro,'" *ASC*, 94–113. Forsythe's papers and music, including the typescript of "Masks," are at the Huntington Library.

2. For more on Arvey, see "*they*, Verna and Billy," *ASC*, 152–81.

3. Still's divorce papers are in the Still-Arvey Papers at UAF. His scrapbooks include a front-page story in the *Pittsburgh Courier.*

4. Letters, John Gray and Florence Cole-Talbert to Still, Still-Arvey Papers, UAF.

5. Still's letters to Dunham are in the Katherine Dunham collection, Southern Illinois University.

6. Carlton Moss (d. 1997) was a writer, filmmaker, and director who was heavily involved in the black unit of the Federal Theater Project in New York City. He was later blacklisted in Hollywood and eventually taught a film class at the University of California—Irvine. See www.ibdb.com for more information.

7. A list of Still's film and TV credits may be found at http://us.imdb.com/name/nm0830238/.

8. Letter, Still to Alain Locke, Aug. 6, 1938, Moorland-Spingarn Research Center, Howard University.

9. Wayne Shirley, "William Grant Still's Choral Ballad *And They Lynched Him on a Tree*," *American Music* 12 (1994): 426–461.

10. Letter, Still to Claude A. Barnett [Associated Negro Press], Feb. 17, 1943, Still-Arvey Papers, UAF. Quoted in Jon Michael Spencer, *The William Grant Still Reader: Essays on Americna Music* (Durham, N.C.: Duke University Press, 1992), 16.

11. Arvey, *In One Lifetime*, 131.

12. Interview, Still with R. Donald Brown, 26.

13. Unidentified interviewer, "'I'm Not Mad at Anyone!' says Artie Shaw," *Music and Rhythm* (Aug., 1941): 6.

CHAPTER 8: *Troubled Island*

1. Operas by the Italian-born American, Gian-Carlo Menotti (1911–2007), trained at the Curtis Institute in Philadelphia, had already been heard at the Met and at NYCO; most of these were composed to his own librettos in English.

2. Other operas by black composers were produced in the intervening years, most notably Scott Joplin's *Treemonisha*. Composed in 1910, it was produced for the first time in 1972, in Atlanta and was soon taken up by opera companies in several other cities.

3. Hughes's scenario and correspondence from Still and Arvey are in the Langston Hughes papers, Beinecke Library, Yale University.

4. The one exception was his setting, working with author Zora Neale Hurston, of melodies she had collected in the Bahamas, done in 1941–2, called *Caribbean Melodies*.

5. Letter, Arna Bontemps to Langston Hughes, Nov. 8, 1936, in Charles H. Nichols, ed., *Arna Bontemps–Langston Hughes Letters, 1925–1967* (New York: Dodd, Mead, 1980), 25.

6. Martin L. Sokol, *The New York City Opera: An American Adventure* (New York: Macmillan, 1981), has little about *Troubled Island*. Information here comes mainly from the Morton Baum and Heinz Condell collections, New York Public Library for the Performing Arts at Lincoln Center. Baum served as its first treasurer; he provided a very useful, detailed account of its early history. Condell was the company's set designer. Essays on *Troubled Island* by Tammy Kernodle, Gayle Murchison, Wayne D. Shirley, and Smith are in the *American Music Research Center Journal*, vol. 13 (2003), a special issue devoted to Still.

7. "Stokowski Plans Variety of Music: Operas, Chamber Music and Youth Concerts Scheduled for City Center Season," *New York Times*, Sept. 12, 1944, 23. Milhaud's *Bolivar* was composed in 1943 and premiered in Paris in 1950.

8. Letter, Still to Newbold Morris, Mar. 29, 1947. Inserted in typescript account of the start of the New York City Center and the NYC Opera, Morton Baum papers, New York Public Library for the Performing Arts at Lincoln Center.

9. Local 802 of the musicians' union decided to discontinue the subsidy it had provided for the company's first five years. The symphony orchestra was discontinued because its conductors could not work with Halasz. Two different ballet companies withdrew from their regular seasons because the City Center threatened to organize its own ballet (later very successful). The director of the very successful repertory drama unit also resigned. One of their few proven money-makers, a Christmas-week run by dancer Paul Draper and

harmonica virtuoso Larry Adler, had to be canceled when both artists were linked to the Communist Party. (A public furor over domestic communism was raging that year, too.)

10. Still [Arvey], "Troubled History of *Troubled Island*," *New York Times*, Mar. 20, 1949, X7.

11. Letter, Howard Taubman to Still, Apr. 18, 1949, Box 33, folder "The New York Times," Still-Arvey Papers, UAF. The full text: "Dear Mr. Still: I cannot tell you how sorry I am that we did not meet, and I hold myself largely responsible. When I heard, on the evening of the premiere of 'The Troubled Island,' that you were leaving the next day I tried hard to get to see you there and then. I assure you we shall get together the next time, either in New York or in California, if I should get out that way again. Sincerely Yours, Howard Taubman." Judith Anne Still continues to espouse the plot theory so strongly that it negatively affected her selection and editing in her self-published documentary history of this opera, *Just Tell the Story–Troubled Island* (Flagstaff, Ariz.: Master Player Library, 2006), making this source unreliable.

12. Baum, typescript account, NYPL, 216.

13. Julius Rudel, telephone interview, June 21, 2005.

14. Jean Dalrymple, *From the Last Row: A Personal History of the New York City Center of Music and Drama* (Clifton, N.J.: J. T. White, 1975), p. 101. Dalrymple was the company's publicist.

15. Olin Downes, *New York Times*, Apr. 1, 1949. A summary of critical response is found in Tammy L. Kernodle, "Arias, Communists, and Conspiracies: The History of Still's *Troubled Island*," *Musical Quarterly* 83 (2000): 487–508.

16. Letter, Carl Van Vechten to Langston Hughes, Apr. 5, 1949, in Emily Bernard, ed., *Remember Me to Harlem: The Letters of Langston Hughes and Carl Van Vechten, 1925–1964* (New York: Alfred A. Knopf, 2001), 257–58. For more on Hughes's response, see Arnold Rampersad, *The Life of Langston Hughes* (New York: Oxford University Press, 1986, vol. 2, 166–67).

CHAPTER 9: Moscow's "Subtle but Effective Hand"

1. For another account of this issue, see Smith, "'Harlem Renaissance Man' Revisited: The Politics of Race and Class in Still's Late Career," *ASC*, 182–212.

2. Quoted in Robert Wilder Blue, "The Inseparable Histories of Julius Rudel and New York City Opera: A Reminiscence," *USOperaweb: Online Magazine Devoted to American Opera*, vol. 2, no. 4 (2002), found on http://www.usoperaweb.com/2002/september/rudel.htm.

3. Interview, Smith and Lance Bowling, with Carlton Moss, Feb. 21, 1993.

4. Still, "Personal Notes," *ASC*, 233.

5. Still, "Politics in Music," *Opera, Concert and Symphony*, August 1947, reprinted in Jon Michael Spencer, ed., *The William Grant Still Reader*, 144–49.

6. The written text of this speech, and a taped version, are at William Grant Still Music. Part of the speech is quoted in *ASC*, p. 169; a page from Still's handwritten text is reproduced as Figure 11 on p. 170.

7. Letters, Charles Seeger to Still, May 6, 1940; Still to Seeger, May 9, 1940, Still-Arvey Papers, UAF.

8. Spencer, *The William Grant Still Reader*, 60.

CHAPTER 10: After the Storm

1. Jon Michael Spencer, "William Grant Still: Eclectic Religionist," *Black Sacred Music: Journal of Theomusicology*, vol. 8, no. 1 (1994): 135–56.

2. Arvey, "New American Opera," *New York Times*, Jan. 23, 1938, 159.

3. Letter, K. W. Bartlett to Still, Jan. 26, 1957, Still-Arvey Papers.

SELECTED WORKS

(Date of composition is given in parentheses, followed by date of
    first performance.)

Although most of Still's unpublished scores may be examined at the
University of Arkansas–Fayetteville, copies of unpublished work (and
most published scores) may be ordered from William Grant Still Music.

Operas

Blue Steel (1934–35)
Troubled Island (1937–41), produced 1949
A Bayou Legend (1941), telecast 1974
A Southern Interlude (1942), also called *Highway 1, U.S.A.*, 1963
Costaso (1949–50), produced 1992
Mota (1951)
The Pillar (1954–5)
Minette Fontaine (1958), 1984

Ballets

La Guiablesse (1926? rev 1932), 1933
Sahdji (1930), 1931 (orchestra, mixed chorus, and solo bass voice)
Miss Sally's Party (1940), 1941

Orchestral Music (Symphonies, Suites)

From the Black Belt (1924), 1927
From the Journal of a Wanderer (1924), 1926
From the Land of Dreams (1924), 1925
Darker America (1924–25), 1926
Levee Land (1925), 1926 (soprano solo)
From the Heart of a Believer (1927)

Africa, Suite for Orchestra (c 1928–35), 1930
Afro-American Symphony (1930), 1931
A Deserted Plantation (1933), 1933 (also pf arr)
Ebon Chronicle (1934), 1936
The Black Man Dances, suite (1935), 1998 (piano solo)
Kaintuck' (1935), 1935, (piano solo, also arr two pianos)
Lenox Avenue (1935, rev. 1937), 1937 (solo piano and narrator;
    also performed as a ballet)
Symphony no. 2 in G Minor, "Song of a New Race" (1936–37), 1937
Can'tcha Line 'Em (1940), 1940
And They Lynched Him on a Tree (1941), 1941 (also choruses and
    vocal soloists)
Old California (1941), 1941
Plain-Chant for America (1940), 1941 (baritone solo; also choral version)
In Memoriam: The Colored Soldiers Who Died for Democracy (1943), 1944
Pages from Negro History (1941), 1944
Festive Overture (1944), 1945
Poem for Orchestra (1944), 1944
Archaic Ritual (1946), 1949
Symphony no. 4, "Autochthonous" (1947), 1951
Symphony no. 5, "Western Hemisphere" (1947, 1958), 1970
Wood Notes (1947), 1948
Little Song that Wanted to Be a Symphony (1953), 1955
The American Scene, 5 suites (1958), arr band, chamber ens.
Symphony no. 3, "The Sunday Symphony" (1958), 1984
Ennanga, (1958), 1958 (solo harp)

Music for Band

From the Delta (1945), 1947
To You, America! (1951), 1952
Folk Suite for Band, 1963 (spiritual arr), 1963
    "Get on Board, Little Children"
    "Deep River"
    "The Old Ark's a Moverin"
    "Sinner, Please Don't Let This Harvest Pass"

Solo Piano Music

Quit Dat Fool'nish (1935), 1935 (also arr for fl and pf, vn and pf,
    sax and pf, orch)
Three Visions (1935), 1936
    "Dark Horseman"

"Summerland" (also arr for small orch and other instrumental
combinations)
"Radiant Pinnacle"
Seven Traceries (1939), 1959

Songs and Choral Music

Breath of a Rose (1928), 1927
Mandy Lou (1927), 1927
Winter's Approach (1927)
Twelve Negro Spirituals, vol. 1 and 2 (1937, 1948)
Song of a City/Rising Tide/Victory Tide (1939), 1939 (chorus with orch;
    also chorus, band, solo voice, and pf)
Here's One (arr 1941), 1942
Caribbean Melodies (1941–42)
Songs of Separation (c. 1945), 1946
    "Idolatry"
    "Poème"
    "Parted"
    "If You Should Go"
    "A Black Pierrot"
Four Octavo Songs
    "Ev'ry Time I Feel the Spirit" (arr 1930), 1953
    "The Blind Man"
    "Toward Distant Shores"
    "Where Shall I Be?" (pub 1977)
Three Rhythmic Spirituals (1956), 1973
Little Folk Suites from the Western Hemisphere #1–5, folksong arr for
    stg quartet and brass quintet

Chamber Music

Incantation and Dance (1941), 1942 (ob and pf)
Suite for Violin and Piano (1943), 1944
Fanfare for the 99th Fighter Squadron (aka Chamber Music for Brass and
    Percussion) (1944), 1945
Pastorela (1946), 1947 (vn and pf)
Danzas de Panama (1948), 1948 (stg quintet, arr stg orch, arr stg quartet)
Miniatures (1948), 1948 (fl, ob, pf)
Romance for Saxophone (1954) (also sax and chamber orch)
Four Indigenous Portraits (1956) (fl and stg quartet, also fl and str orch)
Folk Suites #1–4 (1962), 1984 (various combinations)

FOR FURTHER READING

THE MOST USEFUL of several current books on Still are the present author's *William Grant Still: A Study in Contradictions* (Berkeley and Los Angeles: University of California Press, 2000), hereafter *ASC,* which includes some important sources. Judith Anne Still, Michael J. Dabrishus, and Carolyn L. Quinn's, *William Grant Still: A Bio-Bibliography* (Westport, Conn.: Greenwood Press, 1996), contains extensive information on all of Still's concert music and operas. Jon Michael Spencer, editor of *The William Grant Still Reader: Essays on American Music* (Durham, N.C.: Duke University Press, 1992), anthologizes a number of essays by Still and Arvey and provides a useful introduction. Verna Arvey's, *In One Lifetime* (Fayetteville: University of Arkansas Press, 1984) is a valuable, if opinionated, memoir. Beverly Soll's *I Dream a World: The Operas of William Grant Still* (Fayetteville: University of Arkansas Press, 2005) describes Still's operas in detail. A thematic index is included in Judith Anne Still's self-published revision of Robert Haas's 1972 collection, *William Grant Still and the Fusion of Cultures in American Music* (Flagstaff, Ariz.: Master-Player Library, 1995).

SUGGESTED LISTENING

TRACKS FROM the CDs listed here are also available from standard online download-ing services such as www.rhapsody.com. Other CDs and a list of archival tapes, most of them now digitized, are available from William Grant Still Music, Flagstaff, Arizona, and through Cambria Archives, PO Box 374, Lomita, California, 90717.

Africa, paired with Still's *In Memoriam* and the *Afro-American Symphony.* John Jeter con-ducts the Fort Smith (Arkansas) Symphony. Naxos American Classics 8.559174. LCCN 2005-586631.

Afro-American Symphony (Symphony no. 1) is available in three other versions:
—paired with Still's *Kaintuck', Dismal Swamp,* and music by Olly Wilson. Jindong Cai, Cincinnati Philharmonic Orchestra, Richard Fields, pianist. Centaur CRC 2331, OCLC: 38021002 (my favorite version)
—paired with Duke Ellington, *Suite from "The River."* Neeme Jarvi, Detroit Symphony. Chandos CHAN 9154; OCLC 27960328
—paired with Henry Hadley, *Salome.* Karl Krueger, Royal Philharmonic Orchestra. Library of Congress OMP-106; LCCN: 91-754826

And They Lynched Him on a Tree, paired with *Miss Sally's Party, Wailing Woman, Swanee River,* and other short pieces. Philip Brunelle, Plymouth Music Series of Minnesota, Leigh Morris Chorale. William Warfield, narrator. *Witness, Volume ii,* Collins Classics 14542; OCLC 34773432

Carribbean Suite (arr. from *Caribbean Melodies*), Spirituals, and Art Songs, Videmus, arr. Vivian Taylor, various performers. *More Still-*Videmus, Cambria CD-1112; LCCN 00-527965

Miniatures; Folk Suites 2, 3, 4; Summerland; Quit dat Fool'nish; Romance; Vignettes; Get on Board, Sierra Winds. *Get on Board!* Cambria CD-1083; LC 5882; OCLC: 33383754

Sahdji, Howard Hanson, Eastman-Rochester Orchestra & Chorus. Also music by Robert McBride, Ron Nelson, Lyndol Mitchell, Charles G. Vardell, Jr., and Alberto Ginastera. *Fiesta in Hi-Fi,* Mercury Living Presence 434 324-2; OCLC 30944716

Suite for Violin and Piano, Songs of Separation, Ennanga, Incantation and Dance, Here's One, Summerland, Song for the Lonely, Out of the Silence, Citadel, Lift Every Voice and Sing. Performed by Videmus, Vivian Taylor, director. Robert Honeysucker, baritone; Lynn

Chang, violin; and others. *Works by William Grant Still.* New World Records 80399-2; OCLC: 3268711

Symphony no. 2, "Song of a New Race," paired with William L Dawson's *Negro Folk Symphony,* and Duke Ellington's *Harlem,* Neeme Jarvi, Detroit Symphony. Chandos CHAN 9226; OCLC 29974239

Still as Arranger

Still's arrangement of *Frenesi* for Artie Shaw was released by Victor on 78 rpm recording Victor 26542 in 1940 (OCLC 29304494). WorldCat lists 257 reissues on 45 and 33 1/3 rpm LP records, cassette tape, and CD.

INDEX

CATHERINE PARSONS SMITH is Professor Emerita of Music at the University of Nevada, Reno. She is the author of *Making Music in Los Angeles: Transforming the Popular*, main author of *William Grant Still: A Study in Contradictions*, co-author of *Mary Carr Moore: American Composer*, and author of several music editions and many articles.

The University of Illinois Press
is a founding member of the
Association of American University Presses.

Composed in 9.5/13 Janson Text
with Meta display
by Jim Proefrock
at the University of Illinois Press
Designed by Copenhaver Cumpston
Manufactured by Sheridan Books, Inc.

UNIVERSITY OF ILLINOIS PRESS
1325 South Oak Street
Champaign, IL 61820-6903
www.press.uillinois.edu